Contents

Irish Potato Cake

Ingredients

- 2 cups unsalted butter, softened

- 3 1/2 cups granulated sugar

- 3 eggs

- 1 cup unseasoned mashed potatoes, at room temperature

- 1 cup buttermilk

- 2 cups all purpose flour

- 2 tsp. baking powder

- 1/2 tsp. ground cinnamon

- 1/4 tsp. allspice

- 2 tsp. vanilla extract

- 1 cup chopped pecans

- 1/2 cup whole milk

Directions

1. Preheat the oven to 350°. Spray three 9" round cake pans with non stick cooking spray. In a mixing bowl, add 1 cup butter and 1 1/2 cups granulated sugar. Using a mixer on medium speed, beat for 3 minutes or until the batter is smooth and combined. Add the eggs and mix for 3 minutes. Add the mashed potatoes and buttermilk to the bowl. Mix until well combined.

2. Add the all purpose flour, baking powder, cinnamon, allspice, 1 teaspoon vanilla extract and pecans to the batter. Mix until well combined. Spoon the batter into the prepared pans. Bake for 20 minutes or until a toothpick inserted in the center of the cakes comes out clean. Remove the cakes from the oven and cool the cakes in the pans for 10 minutes. Remove the cakes from the pans and cool completely before frosting.

3. In a sauce pan over medium heat, add 2 cups granulated sugar, 1 teaspoon vanilla extract, 1 cup butter and milk. Stir constantly and cook until the temperature reaches 236° on a candy thermometer. Remove the pan from the heat. Cool the frosting at room temperature. Using a mixer on medium speed, beat until the frosting is light and fluffy. Spread the frosting between the layers and on the top and sides of the cake.

Banana Nut Cake

Ingredients

- 2 1/2 cups cake flour

- 1 1/4 tsp. baking powder

- 1 tsp. salt

- 1 2/3 cups granulated sugar

- 1 1/4 tsp. baking soda

- 1 tsp. ground cinnamon

- 1 1/4 cups mashed ripe banana

- 2/3 cup whole milk

- 2/3 cup vegetable shortening

- 2 eggs

- 8 oz. pkg. cream cheese, softened

- 1/2 cup unsalted butter, softened

- 4 cups powdered sugar

- 1 cup chopped pecans

Directions

1. Preheat the oven to 350°. Spray three 9" round cake pans with non stick cooking spray. In a large mixing bowl, add the cake flour, baking powder, salt, granulated sugar, baking soda and cinnamon. Stir until well combined.

2. Add the mashed banana, milk and vegetable shortening to the dry **Ingredients**. Using a mixer on medium speed, beat for 2 minutes. The batter should be damp at this point. Add the eggs and beat for 1 minute or until the batter is well blended. Spoon the batter into the prepared pans. Bake for 25 minutes or until a toothpick inserted in the center of the cakes comes out clean. Remove the cakes from the oven and cool the cakes in the pans for 10 minutes. Remove the cakes from the pans cool completely before frosting.

3. To prepare the frosting, add the cream cheese, butter and powdered sugar to a mixing bowl. Using a mixer on medium speed, beat for 5 minutes or until the frosting is light and fluffy. Turn the mixer off and fold in the chopped pecans. Spread the frosting between the layers and on the top and sides of the cake.

Southern Banana Cake with Caramel Frosting

Ingredients

- 1 cup unsalted butter, softened

- 2 3/4 cups granulated sugar

- 2 eggs, separated and at room temperature

- 1 tsp. baking soda

- 1/4 cup plus 1 tbs. buttermilk

- 2 cups all purpose flour

- 3 large ripe bananas, peeled and mashed

- 1 cup chopped pecans

- 3/4 cup light brown sugar

- 1 cup evaporated milk

Directions

1. Preheat the oven to 350°. Spray two 8" round cake pans with non stick cooking spray. In a mixing bowl, add 1/2 cup butter and 1 1/2 cups granulated sugar. Using a mixer on medium speed, beat for 3 minutes. Add the egg yolks and beat until smooth and combined.

2. In a small bowl, add the baking soda and buttermilk. Stir until the baking soda dissolves. Add to the mixing bowl along with the all purpose flour. Mix until combined. Turn the mixer off and stir in the bananas and pecans.

3. In a separate mixing bowl, add the egg whites. Using a mixer on medium speed, beat until stiff peaks form. Gently fold the egg whites into the batter. Spoon the batter into the prepared pans. Bake for 30 minutes or until a toothpick inserted in the center of the cakes comes out clean. Remove the cakes from the oven and cool the cakes for 10 minutes in the pans. Remove the cakes from the pans and cool completely before frosting.

4. To make the frosting, add 1 1/4 cups granulated sugar, brown sugar, evaporated milk and 1/2 cup butter to a sauce pan over medium low heat. Stir constantly and cook until the temperature reaches 240° on a candy thermometer. Remove the pan from the heat. Using a hand mixer on medium speed, beat until the frosting is light and fluffy. Frost between the layers and on the top and sides of the cake.

5. The frosting will harden and will not spread if made ahead of time. Do not make the frosting until you are ready to frost the cake.

Carrot Cocoa Cake with Cream Cheese Coconut Frosting

Ingredients

- 2 cups all purpose flour

- 2 cups granulated sugar

- 2 tsp. baking soda

- 1 tsp. salt

- 1/2 cup unsweetened cocoa powder

- 4 eggs

- 1 tsp. vanilla extract

- 1 1/2 cups vegetable oil

- 2 cups grated and peeled carrots

- 8 oz. can crushed pineapple, drained

- 8 oz. cream cheese, softened

- 1/2 cup unsalted butter, softened

- 4 cups powdered sugar

- 1/2 cup sweetened flaked coconut

- 1 cup chopped pecans

Directions

1. Preheat the oven to 350°. Spray three 9" round cake pans with non stick cooking spray. In a mixing bowl, add the all purpose flour, granulated sugar, baking soda, salt and cocoa powder. Stir until combined.

2. In a separate mixing bowl, add the eggs, vanilla extract and vegetable oil. Using a mixer on medium speed, beat until well combined. Turn the mixer to low and add the carrots and pineapple. Mix only until combined. Add the dry **Ingredients** to the batter. Mix until well blended.

3. Spoon the batter into the prepared pans. Bake for 25 minutes or until a toothpick inserted in the center of the cakes comes out clean. Remove the pans from the oven and cool the cakes in the pans for 5 minutes. Remove the cakes from the pans and cool completely before frosting.

4. To make the frosting, add the cream cheese and butter to a mixing bowl. Using a mixer on medium speed, beat until smooth and combined. Add the powdered sugar to the bowl. Mix until combined and the frosting is fluffy. Turn the mixer off and stir in the coconut and pecans. Refrigerate the frosting for 20 minutes. Spread the frosting between the layers and on the top and sides of the cake. Store the cake in the refrigerator.

Supreme Carrot Cake

Ingredients

- 2 cups all purpose flour

- 2 tsp. baking soda

- 1/2 tsp. salt

- 2 tsp. ground cinnamon

- 3 eggs

- 2 cups granulated sugar

- 3/4 cup vegetable oil

- 3/4 cup buttermilk

- 2 tsp. vanilla extract

- 2 cups grated carrot

- 8 oz. can crushed pineapple, drained

- 1 1/3 cups sweetened flaked coconut

- 1 cup chopped pecans

Directions

1. Preheat the oven to 350°. Spray three 9" round cake pans with non stick cooking spray. In a mixing bowl, add the all purpose flour, baking soda, salt and cinnamon. Stir until combined.

2. In a separate mixing bowl, add the eggs, granulated sugar, vegetable oil, buttermilk and vanilla extract. Using a mixer on medium speed, beat for 4 minutes. Turn the mixer speed to low and add the dry **Ingredients**. Mix only until the cake batter is smooth and combined. Turn the mixer off and fold in the carrot, pineapple, coconut and pecans.

3. Spoon the batter into the cake pans. Bake for 25 minutes or until a toothpick inserted in the center of the cakes comes out clean. Remove the cakes from the oven and cool the cakes in the pans for 10 minutes. Remove the cakes from the pans and cool completely before frosting. Frost with your favorite frosting.

Spice Layer Cake

Ingredients

- 1/2 cup plus 1 tsp. unsalted butter, softened

- 1 1/4 cups light brown sugar

- 3 eggs, at room temperature

- 1 3/4 cups all purpose flour

- 2 tsp. baking powder

- 1/2 tsp. baking soda

- 1/4 tsp. salt

- 1 tsp. ground cinnamon

- 1/2 tsp. ground allspice

- 1/2 tsp. ground nutmeg

- 3/4 cup sour cream

- 1/2 cup finely chopped pecans

- 1 oz. unsweetened baking chocolate

- 2/3 cup unsalted butter, softened

- 1/3 cup sour cream

- 1/8 tsp. salt

- 4 1/3 cups powdered sugar

- 1 tsp. vanilla extract

Directions

1. Preheat the oven to 350°. Spray two 8" round cake pans with non stick cooking spray. In a mixing bowl, add 1/2 cup butter and the brown sugar. Using a mixer on medium speed, beat for 5 minutes. Add the eggs and beat for 3 minutes. Add the all purpose flour, baking powder, baking soda, 1/4 teaspoon salt, cinnamon, allspice, nutmeg and 3/4 cup sour cream. Mix until the batter is well combined. Turn the mixer off and stir in the pecans.

2. Spoon the batter into the cake pans. Bake for 25 minutes or until a toothpick inserted in the center of the cakes comes out clean. Remove the cakes from the oven and cool the cakes in the pans for 10 minutes. Remove the cakes from the pans and cool completely before frosting.

3. In a microwavable bowl, add 1 teaspoon butter and the chocolate. Stir every 15 seconds. Cook for 1 minute or until the chocolate and butter melt. Remove the bowl from the microwave and stir until well combined.

4. In a mixing bowl, add 2/3 cup butter, 1/3 cup sour cream and 1/8 teaspoon salt. Using a mixer on medium speed, beat until smooth and creamy. Add the powdered sugar and vanilla extract to the bowl. Mix until the frosting is smooth and combined.

5. Spread the frosting between the layers and on the top and sides of the cake. Drizzle the melted chocolate over the top of the cake. Store the cake in the refrigerator.

Blackberry Layer Cake

Ingredients

- 2 cans blackberries, 15 oz. size

- 3 cups all purpose flour

- 1 3/4 cups unsalted butter, softened

- 2 cups granulated sugar

- 4 eggs

- 4 1/2 tbs. unsweetened baking cocoa

- 1 tbs. plus 1 tsp. baking soda

- 1 tsp. ground allspice

- 1 tsp. ground cinnamon

- 1 tsp. ground cloves

- 2 1/2 tsp. vanilla extract

- 6 cups powdered sugar

- 1/4 cup plus 1 tbs. strong brewed coffee

Directions

1. Preheat the oven to 350°. Spray three 9" round cake pans with non stick cooking spray. Drain the blackberries but save 1/2 cup juice. Add the blackberries and 1/2 cup all purpose flour to a small bowl. Toss until the blackberries are coated in the flour.

2. In a mixing bowl, add 1 cup butter and the granulated sugar. Using a mixer on medium speed, beat for 3 minutes. Add the eggs and beat for 3 minutes. Add the reserved 1/2 cup blackberry liquid, 2 1/2 cups all purpose flour, 3 tablespoons cocoa, baking soda, allspice, cinnamon and cloves. Mix until the batter is smooth and combined. Turn the mixer off and fold in the blackberries and 1 teaspoon vanilla extract.

3. Spoon the batter into the cake pans. Bake for 25 minutes or until a toothpick inserted in the center of the cakes comes out clean. Remove the cakes from the oven. Cool the cakes in the pans for 10 minutes. Remove the cakes from the pans and cool completely before frosting.

4. To make the frosting, add 3/4 cup butter to a mixing bowl. Using a mixer on medium speed, beat for 1 minute. Add the powdered sugar, 1 1/2 tablespoons cocoa, coffee and 1 1/2 teaspoons vanilla extract. Beat for 5 minutes or until the frosting is thick and spreadable. Spread the frosting between the layers and on the top and sides of the cake.

5. Note: You can substitute 2 cups fresh blackberries and 1/2 cup blackberry juice for the canned blackberries if desired.

Blackberry Jam Cake

Ingredients

- 3/4 cup unsalted butter, softened

- 1 cup granulated sugar

- 1/8 tsp. salt

- 3 eggs

- 1 cup blackberry jam

- 1/4 tsp. ground nutmeg

- 1/2 tsp. ground cinnamon

- 2 cups all purpose flour

- 1 tsp. baking soda

- 1/4 cup whole milk

- 1 cup raisins

- 1 cup chopped pecans

- Your favorite vanilla or caramel frosting

Directions

1. Preheat the oven to 350°. Spray three 9" round cake pans with non stick cooking spray. In a mixing bowl, add the butter, granulated sugar and salt. Using a mixer on medium speed, beat for 3 minutes or until the butter is light and fluffy. Add the eggs and beat for 3 minutes. Add the blackberry jam, nutmeg and cinnamon. Mix for 1 minute or until well combined.

2. Reduce the mixer speed to low. Add the all purpose flour, baking soda and milk. Mix for 2 minutes or until the batter is well combined. Turn the mixer off and stir in the raisins and pecans. Pour the batter into the cake pans. Bake for 20 minutes or until a toothpick inserted in the center of the cakes comes out clean. Remove the cakes from the oven and cool the cakes in the pans for 10 minutes. Remove the cakes from the pans and cool completely before frosting.

3. You can frost with vanilla or caramel icing if desired. This cake is good plain or dusted with powdered sugar. If you want to serve this cake without frosting, bake the cake in a 9 x 13 baking pan.

Strawberry Jam Cake

Ingredients

- 1 cup vegetable shortening

- 6 cups granulated sugar

- 3 eggs

- 3 cups all purpose flour

- 1 tsp. ground cloves

- 1 tsp. ground cinnamon

- 1 tsp. ground allspice

- 1 tsp. ground nutmeg

- 1 tsp. baking soda

- 1 cup buttermilk

- 12 oz. jar strawberry preserves

- 2 cups chopped pecans

- 1 cup seedless raisins

- 2 cups unsalted butter

- 2 cups evaporated milk

- 2 tsp. vanilla extract

Directions

1. Preheat the oven to 350°. Spray three 9" round cake pans with non stick cooking spray. In a mixing bowl, add the vegetable shortening and 2 cups granulated sugar. Using a mixer on medium speed, beat for 4 minutes. Add the eggs and beat for 3 minutes. Add 2 3/4 cups all purpose flour, cloves, cinnamon, allspice, nutmeg, baking soda and buttermilk. Mix until the batter is smooth and combined. Turn the mixer off and stir in the strawberry preserves.

2. In a small bowl, add 1/4 cup all purpose flour, pecans and raisins. Toss until combined and add to the cake batter. Stir until combined. Pour the batter into the cake pans. Bake for 20 minutes or until a toothpick inserted in the center of the cakes comes out clean. Remove the cakes from the oven and cool the cakes in the pans for 10 minutes. Remove the cakes from the pans and cool completely before frosting.

3. To make the frosting, add 4 cups granulated sugar, butter and evaporated milk to a dutch oven over medium heat. Stir constantly and bring the frosting to a boil. Place a lid on the pan for 3 minutes. Remove the lid from the pan. Stir constantly and cook until the frosting reaches 234° on a candy thermometer. Remove the pan from the heat and add the vanilla extract. Do not stir the vanilla extract into the frosting at this point. Cool the frosting for 10 minutes.

4. Using a hand mixer, beat the frosting for 8 minutes or until the frosting is smooth and spreadable. Spread the frosting between the layers and on the top and sides of the cake.

Walnut Spice Layer Cake

Ingredients

- 1 1/2 cups water

- 1 cup chopped black walnuts

- 1/2 cup vegetable shortening

- 2 cups light brown sugar

- 3 eggs, separated and at room temperature

- 3 cups all purpose flour

- 1 tbs. baking powder

- 1/2 tsp. salt

- 1 3/4 tsp. ground cinnamon

- 1/2 tsp. ground nutmeg

- 1/2 tsp. ground cloves

- 1 cup plus 1 tbs. whole milk

- 1 cup unsalted butter, softened

- 7 1/2 cups powdered sugar

- 1/8 tsp. salt

- 2 1/2 tsp. vanilla extract

Directions

1. In a sauce pan over medium heat, add the water. When the water is boiling, add the black walnuts. Boil the walnuts for 3 minutes. Remove the pan from the heat and drain all the water from the walnuts.

2. In a mixing bowl, add the vegetable shortening. Using a mixer on medium speed, beat for 1 minute. Add the brown sugar and beat for 3 minutes. Add the egg yolks and beat for 3 minutes. Add 2 3/4 cups all purpose flour, baking powder, 1/2 teaspoon salt, 1/2 teaspoon cinnamon, nutmeg, cloves and 3/4 cup milk. Mix until the batter is smooth and combined. Turn the mixer off.

3. Add the walnuts and 1/4 cup all purpose flour to a small bowl. Toss until the walnuts are coated in the flour. Fold the walnuts into the cake batter. In a mixing bowl, add the egg whites. Using a mixer on medium speed, beat until stiff peaks form. Fold the egg whites into the cake batter.

4. Preheat the oven to 350°. Spray three 9" round cake pans with non stick cooking spray. Spoon the batter into the cake pans. Bake for 25 minutes or until a toothpick inserted in the center of the cakes comes out clean. Remove the cakes from the oven and cool the cakes for 10 minutes in the pans. Remove the cakes from the pans and cool completely before frosting.

5. To make the frosting, add the butter to a mixing bowl. Using a mixer on medium speed, beat for 1 minute. Add the powdered sugar, 1 1/4 teaspoons cinnamon, 1/8 teaspoon salt, 1/4 cup plus 1 tablespoon milk and the vanilla extract. Beat for 5 minutes or until the frosting is thick and spreadable.

6. Spread the frosting between the layers and on the top and sides of the cake. Let the cake sit for 3 hours before serving.

Peppermint Candy Cake

- 2/3 cup vegetable shortening

- 1 3/4 cups granulated sugar

- 3 cups cake flour

- 3 1/2 tsp. baking powder
- 1/2 tsp. salt
- 1 1/3 cups whole milk
- 1 tsp. vanilla extract
- 4 egg whites, at room temperature
- 1 cup crushed peppermint candies

Peppermint Filling

1/3 cup unsalted butter

- 1 cup granulated sugar
- 1/3 cup whole milk
- 1/2 tsp. peppermint extract

Boiled Frosting

1 1/2 cups granulated sugar

- 1/2 cup water
- 1/2 tsp. cream of tartar
- 1/8 tsp. salt
- 4 egg whites, at room temperature
- 1/2 tsp. almond extract

Directions

1. Preheat the oven to 350°. Spray three 8" round cake pans with non stick cooking spray. To make the cake batter, add the vegetable shortening and granulated sugar to a mixing bowl. Using a mixer on medium speed, beat for 3 minutes. Add the cake flour, baking powder, salt, milk and vanilla extract. Mix until the cake batter is combined.

2. In a separate mixing bowl, add the egg whites. Using a mixer on medium speed, beat until stiff peaks form. Fold the egg whites into the cake batter. Spoon the batter into the prepared pans. Bake for 25 minutes or until a toothpick inserted in the center of the cakes comes out clean. Remove the cakes from the oven and cool for 10 minutes in the pan. Using a fork, poke holes at 1" intervals in the cakes. Remove the cakes from the pan and cool completely before filling and frosting.

3. To make the peppermint filling, add the butter, granulated sugar, milk and peppermint extract to a sauce pan over medium low heat. Stir constantly and bring the filling to a boil. Boil for 1 minute and remove the pan from the heat. Remove the pan from the heat and cool before using .

4. To make the frosting, add the granulated sugar, water, cream of tartar and salt to a sauce pan over medium heat. Stir constantly and cook until the mixture turns clear. Once the mixture is clear, do not

stir. Cook until the temperature reaches 240° on a candy thermometer. Remove the pan from the heat.

5. Add the egg whites to a mixing bowl. Using a mixer on medium speed, beat until soft peaks form. With the mixer running, slowly add the hot sugar syrup. Mix until stiff peaks form. Add the almond extract and mix until combined.

6. To assemble the cake, place one layer on a serving plate. Spread 1/3 of the peppermint filling over the cake. Sprinkle 1/4 cup peppermint candies over the cake layer. Place another cake layer over filling. Spread 1/3 of the peppermint filling over the cake. Sprinkle 1/4 cup peppermint candies over the filling. Place the final layer on the cake. Frost the top and sides of the cake with the boiled frosting. Sprinkle 1/2 cup peppermint candies over the top.

Lady Baltimore Cake

- 3/4 cup vegetable shortening

- 2 cups granulated sugar

- 3 cups cake flour

- 1 tbs. baking powder

- 1/2 tsp. salt

- 1/2 cup whole milk

- 1/2 cup water

- 1 tsp. vanilla extract

- 6 egg whites, at room temperature

Filling

1 1/2 cups granulated sugar

- 1/8 tsp. cream of tartar

- 1/4 cup plus 2 tbs. water

- 2 egg whites, at room temperature

- 1 tsp. vanilla extract

- 1/2 tsp. lemon extract

- 1 1/2 cups chopped pecans

- 1 cup chopped raisins

- 1 cup chopped dried figs

Frosting

1 cup granulated sugar

- 1 egg white, at room temperature

- 1 tbs. light corn syrup

- 1/8 tsp. salt

- 3 tbs. cold water

- 1 tsp. vanilla extract

- 10 walnut halves

Directions

1. To make the cake batter, add the vegetable shortening to a mixing bowl. Using a mixer on medium speed, beat for 30 seconds. With the mixer running, slowly add the granulated sugar. Mix for 2 minutes. Add the cake flour, baking powder, salt, milk, water and vanilla extract. Mix only until well combined and the batter is smooth .

2. In a separate mixing bowl, add the egg whites. Using a mixer on medium speed, beat until stiff peaks form. Gently fold the egg whites into the cake batter. Spray three 9" round cake pans with non stick cooking spray. Spoon the batter into the cake pans.

3. Preheat the oven to 350°. Bake for 25 minutes or until a toothpick inserted in the center of the cakes comes out clean. Remove the cakes from the oven and cool the cakes for 10 minutes in the pans. Remove the cakes from the pans and cool completely before filling and frosting.

4. To make the filling, add the granulated sugar, cream of tartar and water to a sauce pan over medium heat. Stir constantly and cook until the mixture comes to a boil. Continue stirring and cook until the filling reaches 240° on a candy thermometer. Remove the pan from the heat.

5. Add the egg whites to a mixing bowl. Using a mixer on medium speed, beat until the egg whites are foamy. With the mixer running, slowly add the hot syrup to the egg whites. When all the syrup has been added, turn the mixer to high. Beat until stiff peaks form. Add the vanilla and lemon extract to the bowl. Mix only until combined. Turn the mixer off. Gently fold in the pecans, raisins and figs.

6. To make the frosting, add the granulated sugar, egg white, corn syrup, salt and cold water to the top of a double boiler. Using a hand mixer on medium speed, beat for 30 seconds or until all the **Ingredients** are well combined. Continue mixing for 7 minutes or until stiff peaks form. Remove the pan from the heat and mix in the vanilla extract. The frosting should be hot.

7. Run cold water in your sink to a depth of about 2/3 up the side of the pan. Place the pan in the cold water making sure no water gets in the pan. Cool the frosting for 5 minutes. The frosting will still be slightly warm when you frost the cake. Do not make the frosting until the cake has cooled and the filling is ready.

8. When ready to assemble the cake, reserve 1/4 cup filling for the top of the cake. Spread the remaining filling between the layers. Frost the top and sides of the cake with the frosting. Spoon 1/4 cup reserved filling in the center on top of the cake. Place the walnut halves around the cake and serve.

Lord Baltimore Cake

- 3/4 cup unsalted butter, softened
- 1 1/4 cups granulated sugar
- 8 egg yolks
- 2 1/4 cups cake flour
- 1 tbs. baking powder
- 1/2 tsp. salt
- 3/4 cup whole milk
- 1/2 tsp. lemon extract

Filling and Frosting

1 1/2 cups granulated sugar

- 1 tbs. light corn syrup
- 1/2 cup water
- 2 egg whites, at room temperature
- 1/4 tsp. orange juice
- 2 tsp. lemon juice
- 12 candied cherries, chopped
- 1/2 cup macaroon cookies, crushed
- 1/2 cup toasted almonds, chopped
- 1/2 cup chopped pecans

Directions

1. To make the cake batter, add the butter and granulated sugar to a mixing bowl. Using a mixer on medium speed, beat for 3 minutes. The mixture should be smooth and creamy. In a separate mixing bowl, add the egg yolks. Using a mixer on medium speed, beat for 4 minutes or until the egg yolks are light and lemon colored. Add the egg yolks to the butter and granulated sugar. Mix until combined.

2. Add the cake flour, baking powder, salt, milk and lemon extract to the bowl. Mix only until combined. Preheat the oven to 350°. Spray three 9" round cake pans with non stick cooking spray. Spoon the batter into the cake pans. Bake for 20 minutes or until a toothpick inserted in the center of the cakes comes out clean. Remove the cakes from the oven and cool the cakes in the pans for 10 minutes. Remove the cakes from the pans and cool completely before filling and frosting.

3. To make the filling and frosting, add the granulated sugar, corn syrup and water to a sauce pan over low heat. Stir frequently and cook until the temperature reaches 240° on a candy thermometer. Remove the pan from the heat.

4. Add the egg whites to a mixing bowl. Using a mixer on medium speed, beat until soft peaks form. Slowly add the syrup from the pan to the bowl. Beat until well combined and stiff peaks form. Turn the mixer off and gently fold in the orange juice, lemon juice, candied cherries, macaroon crumbs, almonds and pecans.

5. Place the filling and frosting between the cake layers and on the sides and top of the cake.

Fresh Fig Layer Cake

Ingredients

- 1/3 cup unsalted butter, softened

- 1 1/3 cups granulated sugar

- 1 egg

- 2 cups all purpose flour

- 1/3 tsp. salt

- 2 tsp. baking powder

- 1 cup whole milk

- 1/2 cup finely chopped fresh figs

- 2 2/3 cups chopped fresh figs

- 1/3 cup water

- 1 tbs. lemon juice

Directions

1. Preheat the oven to 350°. Spray two 9" round cake pans with non stick cooking spray. In a mixing bowl, add the butter and 1 cup granulated sugar. Using a mixer on medium speed, beat for 2 minutes. Add the eggs and beat for 2 minutes. Add 1 1/2 cups all purpose flour, salt, baking powder and milk. Mix only until combined. Turn the mixer off.

2. In a small bowl, add 1/2 cup all purpose flour and 1/2 cup figs. Toss until the figs are coated in the flour. Fold the figs into the cake batter. Spoon the batter into the prepared pans. Bake for 30 minutes or until a toothpick inserted in the center of the cakes comes out clean. Remove the cakes from the oven and cool the cakes for 10 minutes in the pans. Remove the cakes from the pans and cool completely before filling.

3. To prepare the filling, add 2 2/3 cups figs, 1/3 cup granulated sugar, water and lemon juice to a sauce pan over medium heat. Stir until well combined and bring the figs to a boil. Reduce the heat to medium low. Stir constantly and cook about 20 minutes or until the figs thicken. Remove the pan

from the heat.

4. Cool the filling for 10 minutes. Spread the warm filling between the layers and on the top and sides of the cake. Let the cake sit for 4 hours before serving.

Mandarin Orange Pineapple Cake

Ingredients

- 18 oz. box white cake mix

- 4 eggs

- 1/2 cup vegetable oil

- 11 oz. can mandarin oranges

- 20 oz. can crushed pineapple

- 12 oz. carton Cool Whip, thawed

- 4 serving size instant vanilla pudding mix

Directions

1. Preheat the oven to 350°. Spray two 9" round cake pans with non stick cooking spray. In a large mixing bowl, add the cake mix, eggs, vegetable oil and the mandarin oranges with juice. Using a mixer on medium speed, beat for 4 minutes. The batter should be combined and fluffy. Pour the batter into the prepared cake pans. Bake for 20 minutes or until a toothpick inserted in the center of the cakes comes out clean. Remove the cakes from the oven and cool the cakes in the pans for 10 minutes. Remove the cakes from the pans and cool completely before frosting.

2. For the frosting, add the pineapple with juice, Cool Whip and dry vanilla pudding mix to a mixing bowl. Stir until well combined and fluffy.

3. Cut each cake layer into two layers. Place one layer down on a serving plate. Spoon about 1/2 cup Cool Whip frosting on the layer. Repeat with the remaining layers and frost the top as desired. Garnish with mandarin orange slices or pineapple tidbits if desired. Refrigerate until ready to serve. Store the cake in the refrigerator.

Pineapple Meringue Cake

Ingredients

- 1/2 cup unsalted butter

- 2 1/4 cups granulated sugar

- 4 eggs, separated and at room temperature

- 2 cups all purpose flour

- 3/4 cup whole milk

- 1 cup sweetened flaked coconut

- 1 cup whipping cream

- 8 oz. can crushed pineapple, drained

Directions

1. Preheat the oven to 325°. Spray two 8" round cake pans with non stick cooking spray. In a mixing bowl, add the butter and 1 cup granulated sugar. Using a mixer on medium speed, beat for 3 minutes. Add the egg yolks and beat for 3 minutes. Add the all purpose flour and milk. Mix until the batter is smooth and combined. Spread the batter into the prepared pans.

2. In a mixing bowl, add the egg whites. Using a mixer on medium speed, beat until the egg whites are foamy. With the mixer running, slowly add 3/4 cup granulated sugar. Beat until stiff peaks form. Turn the mixer off and fold in the coconut. Spread the meringue over the top of the cake batter in the pans. Make sure the cake batter and meringue are spread all the way to the sides of the pans.

3. Bake for 30 minutes or until the cakes are done and the meringue lightly browned. Remove the cakes from the oven and cool the cakes in the pans for 10 minutes. Remove the cakes from the pans and cool completely.

4. In a mixing bowl, add the whipping cream. Using a mixer on medium speed, beat until the cream is foamy. With the mixer running, slowly add 1/2 cup granulated sugar. Beat until stiff peaks form. Turn the mixer off and fold in the pineapple.

5. Place one layer, meringue side up, on a serving platter. Place the second layer, meringue side down, over the first layer. Spread the whipped cream over the top of the cake. Store the cake in the refrigerator.

Rocky Mountain Coconut Cake

Ingredients

- 1 cup unsalted butter, softened

- 3 1/2 cups granulated sugar

- 4 eggs

- 3 cups all purpose flour

- 1 tbs. baking powder

- 1/4 tsp. salt

- 1 cup whole milk

- 1 tsp. vanilla extract

- 1/2 cup water

- 2 egg whites

- 3 1/2 cups sweetened grated coconut

- 2 cups chopped raisins

- 1 cup currants

- 1 cup chopped almonds

Directions

1. To make the cake batter, add the butter to a mixing bowl. Using a mixer on medium speed, beat for 30 seconds. With the mixer running, slowly add 2 cups granulated sugar. Mix until smooth and combined. Add the eggs, one at a time, to the bowl. Mix until well combined. Add the all purpose flour, baking powder, salt, milk and vanilla extract. Mix only until well combined and the batter is smooth.

2. Spray three 9" round cake pans with non stick cooking spray. Spoon the batter into the cake pans. Preheat the oven to 350°. Bake for 25 minutes or until a toothpick inserted in the center of the cakes comes out clean. Remove the cakes from the oven and cool the cakes for 10 minutes in the pans. Remove the cakes from the pans and cool completely before filling.

3. To make the filling, add 1 1/2 cups granulated sugar and water to a sauce pan over medium heat. Stir constantly and cook until the syrup comes to a full rolling boil. Remove the pan from the heat.

4. Add the egg whites to a mixing bowl. Using a mixer on medium speed, beat until the egg whites are foamy. With the mixer running, slowly add the hot syrup to the egg whites. When all the syrup has been added, turn the mixer to high. Beat until stiff peaks form and the filling is thick enough to spread. Turn the mixer off. Gently fold in 2 1/2 cups coconut, raisins, currants and almonds.

5. Place the filling between the cake layers. The sides of the cake are not covered. Sprinkle 1 cup grated coconut over the top of the cake.

Dried Apple Cake

Ingredients

- 3 cups dried apples

- 1 1/2 cups molasses

- 1 cup unsalted butter, softened

- 1 1/2 cups granulated sugar

- 2 eggs

- 1 tsp. baking soda

- 1 cup buttermilk

- 4 cups all purpose flour

- 2 tsp. baking powder

- 1 tsp. ground cinnamon

- 1 tsp. ground cloves

- 1 tsp. vanilla extract

- 1 cup raisins

- 1 cup chopped pecans

- 1 1/2 cups peach preserves

- 1 1/2 cups pear preserves

Directions

1. In a mixing bowl, add the apples. Add cold water to cover the apples. Let the apples sit overnight in the refrigerator. Drain any remaining water from the apples. Add the apples to a sauce pan over medium heat. Add the molasses to the apples. Stir frequently and cook until the molasses absorb into the apples or about 20 minutes. Remove the pan from the heat and set aside to cool.

2. In a mixing bowl, add the butter and granulated sugar. Using a mixer on medium speed, beat for 3 minutes. Add the eggs and beat for 3 minutes. In a small bowl, add the baking soda and buttermilk. Stir until the baking soda dissolves.

3. Add the baking soda mixture, all purpose flour, baking powder, cinnamon, cloves and vanilla extract to the bowl. Mix only until combined. Turn the mixer off and stir in the apples, raisins and pecans.

4. Spray three 9" round cake pans with non stick cooking spray. Spoon the batter into the pans. Preheat the oven to 350°. Bake for 30 minutes or until a toothpick inserted in the center of the cakes comes out clean. Remove the cakes from the oven and cool the cakes in the pans for 10 minutes. Remove the cakes from the pans and cool completely.

5. In a bowl, add the peach and pear preserves. Stir until combined. Spread the preserves between the layers and over the top of the cake.

Applesauce Stack Cake

Ingredients

- 3/4 cup vegetable shortening

- 1 cup granulated sugar

- 1 cup molasses

- 3 eggs

- 4 cups all purpose flour

- 1/2 tsp. baking soda

- 1 tsp. salt

- 1 tsp. ground ginger

- 1 cup whole milk

- 3 cups applesauce

- Ground cinnamon to taste

Directions

1. This cake needs to sit for 3 days before serving. Preheat the oven to 375°. Spray six 9" round cake pans with non stick cooking spray. In a mixing bowl, add the vegetable shortening. Using a mixer on medium speed, beat for 2 minutes. Add the granulated sugar and molasses. Beat for 3 minutes. Add the eggs and beat for 2 minutes.

2. Add the all purpose flour, baking soda, salt, ginger and milk. Mix until the batter is smooth and combined. Spoon the batter into the cake pans. Bake for 16 minutes or until a toothpick inserted in the center of the cakes comes out clean. Remove the cakes from the oven and immediately remove the cakes from the pans. Cool the cakes completely before assembling.

3. To stack the cake, place a layer on a serving platter. Spread 1/2 cup applesauce over the layer. Repeat until all the layers are stacked. Sprinkle cinnamon to taste over the applesauce on the top layer. Let the cake sit for 3 days covered before serving.

Old Fashioned Apple Stack Cake

Ingredients

- 1/2 cup vegetable shortening

- 1 3/4 cups granulated sugar

- 1/2 cup plus 2 tbs. buttermilk

- 3/4 tsp. baking soda

- 1 tbs. baking powder

- 1/4 tsp. salt

- 1 3/4 tsp. ground ginger

- 3 3/4 cups all purpose flour

- 4 cups dried apples

- 2 2/3 cups water

Directions

1. This cake needs to sit for 3 days before serving. Preheat the oven to 400°. In a mixing bowl, add the vegetable shortening. Using a mixer on medium speed, beat for 2 minutes. Add 1 1/4 cups granulated sugar and beat for 3 minutes. Add the buttermilk, baking soda, baking powder, salt, ginger and all purpose flour. Mix until well combined. The dough will be very stiff.

2. Divide the dough into 5 equal portions. Spray 5 baking sheets with non stick cooking spray. Place each portion on a baking sheet. Pat the dough into a 9" circle. Bake for 6-8 minutes or until the cake is golden brown. Remove the baking sheets from the oven and carefully remove the cakes from the baking sheets. Cool the cakes completely before assembling.

3. To make the filling, add the dried apples and water to a sauce pan over medium heat. Bring the apples to a boil and reduce the heat to low. Stir occasionally and simmer the apples for 30 minutes. The apples should be very tender when ready. Remove the pan from the heat and stir in 1/2 cup granulated sugar. Stir until combined and mash the apples slightly with a fork. The mixture should resemble a chunky applesauce. Cool the apples completely before using.

4. To stack the cake, place a layer on the serving platter. Spread 3/4 cup apple filling over the layer. Repeat until all the layers are stacked. The top layer will not have filling on top. Let the cake sit for 3 days covered before serving.

Southern Lemon Layer Cake

- 2 cups all purpose flour

- 1/2 tsp. cream of tartar

- 1 1/2 tsp. baking powder

- 8 eggs, separated and at room temperature

- 2 cups granulated sugar

- 2 tsp. grated lemon zest

- 2 tbs. lemon juice

- 1/8 tsp. salt

Lemon Jelly Filling

4 egg yolks

- 1 1/3 cups granulated sugar

- 2 1/2 tsp. grated lemon zest

- 1/4 cup plus 1 1/2 tbs. lemon juice

- 1/4 cup unsalted butter

Lemon Orange Frosting

1/3 cup unsalted butter, softened

- 4 cups powdered sugar

- 3 tbs. grated orange zest

- 2 1/2 tbs. orange juice

- 1 1/2 tsp. grated lemon zest

- 1 tbs. plus 1 tsp. lemon juice

- 1/2 cup sweetened flaked coconut

Directions

1. To make the cake batter, add the all purpose flour, cream of tartar and baking powder to a small bowl. Stir until combined. Add the egg yolks to a large mixing bowl. Using a mixer on medium speed, beat for 4 minutes. Add the granulated sugar and beat until the egg yolks are light and lemon colored. Add the lemon zest and lemon juice to the bowl. Mix until combined.

2. Add the egg whites and salt to a mixing bowl. Using a mixer on medium speed, beat until soft peaks form. Turn the mixer off. Add the egg yolks and dry **Ingredients** to the egg whites. Fold the egg yolks and dry **Ingredients** until the cake batter is well combined.

3. Spray two 9" round cake pans with non stick cooking spray. Spoon the batter into the cake pans. Preheat the oven to 350°. Bake for 25 minutes or until a toothpick inserted in the center of the cakes comes out clean. Remove the cakes from the oven and cool the cakes for 10 minutes in the pans. Remove the cakes from the pans and cool completely .

4. To make the filling, add the egg yolks, granulated sugar, lemon zest and lemon juice to a double boiler over medium heat. Stir constantly and cook until the filling begins to boil. Add the butter to the pan. Stir constantly and cook for 20 minutes. Remove the pan from the heat and cool completely before using.

5. To make the frosting, add the butter to a mixing bowl. Using a mixer on medium speed, beat until the butter is light and fluffy. Add the powdered sugar, orange zest, orange juice, lemon zest, lemon juice and coconut to the bowl. Mix until the frosting is combined and fluffy.

6. Split the cooled cake layers in half horizontally. Spread the lemon jelly filling between the layers. Frost the top and sides of the cake with the frosting.

Coconut Cream Cake

Ingredients

- 1 cup unsalted butter, softened

- 2 cups plus 1 tsp. granulated sugar

- 3 eggs, at room temperature

- 3 cups all purpose flour

- 2 tsp. baking powder

- 1 cup whole milk

- 2 tsp. vanilla extract

- 1/2 tsp. butter flavoring

- 1/2 cup water

- 2 cups whipping cream

- 1/2 cup powdered sugar

- 1 tsp. coconut extract

- 2 drops butter flavoring

- 3 cups sweetened flaked coconut

Directions

1. Preheat the oven to 350°. Spray three 9" round cake pans with non stick cooking spray. In a mixing bowl, add the butter and 2 cups granulated sugar. Using a mixer on medium speed, beat for 3 minutes. Add the eggs and beat for 3 minutes. Add the all purpose flour, baking powder, milk, 1 teaspoon vanilla extract and 1/2 teaspoon butter flavoring. Mix only until the batter is combined.

2. Spoon the batter into the cake pans. Bake for 25 minutes or until a toothpick inserted in the center of the cakes comes out clean. Remove the cakes from the oven and cool the cakes for 10 minutes in the pan. Remove the cakes from the pans and cool completely before frosting.

3. Do not make the frosting and sugar syrup until you are ready to frost the cake. In a sauce pan over medium heat, add the water and 1 teaspoon granulated sugar. Stir constantly and bring the syrup to a boil. Boil for 3 minutes. Remove the pan from the heat. Spoon the syrup over the cake layers.

4. In a mixing bowl, add the whipping cream, powdered sugar, 1 teaspoon vanilla extract, coconut extract and 2 drops butter flavoring. Using a mixer on medium speed, beat until soft peaks form. Turn the mixer off and fold in the coconut. Spread the frosting between the layers and on the top and sides of the cake. Store the cake in the refrigerator.

Orange Coconut Cake

Ingredients

- 3 cups grated unsweetened coconut

- 1 tbs. grated orange zest

- 2 tbs. orange juice

- 2 tbs. minced orange

- 3 1/2 cups plus 2 tbs. granulated sugar

- 4 eggs

- 1 cup hot milk, at 140°

- 1/4 cup vegetable oil

- 2 cups cake flour

- 2 tsp. baking powder

- 1/2 tsp. salt

- 1/2 tsp. almond extract

- 1/2 cup water

- 2 egg whites, at room temperature

- 1 tsp. vanilla extract

Directions

1. In a mixing bowl, add the coconut, orange zest, orange juice, orange and 2 tablespoons granulated sugar. Stir until combined. Cover the bowl and refrigerate for 12 hours.

2. In a mixing bowl, add the eggs. Using a mixer on medium speed, beat until the eggs are frothy. Add 2 cups granulated sugar to the eggs. Beat for 4 minutes or until the mixture is thick and lemon colored. Add the milk and vegetable oil to the bowl. Mix until combined.

3. Add the cake flour, baking powder, salt and almond extract to the bowl. Mix only until combined. Spray three 8" round cake pans with non stick cooking spray. Preheat the oven to 350°. Spoon the batter into the cake pans. Bake for 20 minutes or until a toothpick inserted in the center of the cakes comes out clean. Remove the cakes from the oven and cool the cakes in the pans for 10 minutes. Remove the cakes from the pans and cool completely before frosting.

4. To make the frosting, add 1 1/2 cups granulated sugar and water to a sauce pan over medium heat. Stir constantly until the syrup boils. Do not stir once the syrup is boiling. Cook until the temperature reaches 240° on a candy thermometer. Remove the pan from the heat.

5. In a mixing bowl, add the egg whites. Using a mixer on medium speed, beat until the egg whites are foamy. With the mixer running, slowly pour the syrup over the egg whites. Beat until stiff peaks form. Add the vanilla extract and mix until the frosting is thick and spreadable.

6. To assemble the cake, place one layer on a cake platter. Spread frosting over the layer. Spread 3/4 cup orange coconut mixture over the frosting. Place another layer on the cake. Spread frosting over the layer. Spread 3/4 cup orange coconut mixture over the frosting. Place the final layer on the cake. Spread the remaining orange coconut mixture over the top. Frost the top and sides of the cake with the remaining frosting. Store the cake in the refrigerator.

Pineapple Filled Coconut Cake

- 1 cup vegetable shortening

- 2 cups granulated sugar

- 4 eggs

- 3 cups sifted cake flour

- 2 1/2 tsp. baking powder

- 1/2 tsp. salt

- 1 cup whole milk

- 1 tsp. almond extract

- 1 tsp. vanilla extract

Pineapple Filling

3 tbs. all purpose flour

- 1/2 cup granulated sugar

- 20 oz. can crushed pineapple

- 2 tbs. unsalted butter

Boiled Frosting

1 1/2 cups granulated sugar

- 1/2 cup water

- 1/2 tsp. cream of tartar

- 1/8 tsp. salt

- 4 egg whites, at room temperature

- 1/2 tsp. almond extract

Directions

1. To make the cake batter, add the vegetable shortening and granulated sugar to a mixing bowl. Using a mixer on medium speed, beat for 3 minutes. Add the eggs and beat for 3 minutes.

2. Turn the mixer to low speed. Add the cake flour, baking powder, salt, milk, almond and vanilla extract. Mix only until the batter is combined. Preheat the oven to 375°. Spray three 9" round cake pans with non stick cooking spray. Spoon the cake batter into the pans. Bake for 20 minutes or until a toothpick inserted in the center of the cakes comes out clean. Remove the cakes from the oven and cool in the pans for 10 minutes. Remove the cakes from the pans and cool completely before filling and frosting.

3. To make the filling, add the all purpose flour, granulated sugar, pineapple with juice and butter to a sauce pan over medium heat. Stir constantly and cook until the filling thickens and bubbles. Remove the pan from the heat and cool completely before using .

4. To make the frosting, add the granulated sugar, water, cream of tartar and salt to a sauce pan over medium heat. Stir constantly and cook until the mixture turns clear. Once the mixture is clear, do not stir. Cook until the temperature reaches 240° on a candy thermometer. Remove the pan from the heat.

5. Add the egg whites to a mixing bowl. Using a mixer on medium speed, beat until soft peaks form. With the mixer running, slowly add the hot sugar syrup. Mix until stiff peaks form. Add the almond extract and mix until combined.

6. Spread the filling between the layers. Frost the top and sides of the cake with the frosting.

Southern Orange Cake

Ingredients

- 2 1/2 cups all purpose flour

- 1 1/2 cups granulated sugar

- 1 1/2 tsp. baking soda

- 1/4 tsp. salt

- 1 1/2 cups buttermilk

- 1 cup unsalted butter, softened

- 1/4 cup vegetable shortening

- 3 eggs

- 1 1/2 tsp. vanilla extract

- 2 tbs. grated orange zest

- 1 cup golden seedless raisins, chopped

- 1/2 cup finely chopped pecans

- 4 1/2 cups powdered sugar

- 5 tbs. orange juice

Directions

1. In a mixing bowl, add the all purpose flour, granulated sugar, baking soda, salt, buttermilk, 1/2 cup butter, vegetable shortening, eggs, vanilla extract and 1 tablespoon orange zest. Using a mixer on low speed, beat for 30 seconds. Turn the mixer to high speed and beat for 3 minutes. The batter should be smooth and combined. Turn the mixer off and stir in the raisins and pecans.

2. Spray three 9" round cake pans with non stick cooking spray. Spoon the batter into the cake pans. Preheat the oven to 350°. Bake for 30 minutes or until a toothpick inserted in the center of the cakes comes out clean. Remove the cakes from the oven and cool the cakes for 10 minutes in the pans. Remove the cakes from the pans and cool completely.

3. To make the frosting, add 1/2 cup butter to a mixing bowl. Using a mixer on medium speed, beat until the butter is light and fluffy. Add the powdered sugar, 1 tablespoon orange zest and 4 tablespoons orange juice to the bowl. Mix until the frosting is combined and fluffy. Add the remaining tablespoon orange juice if needed to make a fluffy frosting. Spread the frosting between the layers and on the top and sides of the cake.

Southern Rum Layer Cake

Ingredients

- 1 cup unsalted butter, softened

- 2 cups granulated sugar

- 3 1/2 cups cake flour

- 1 tbs. baking powder

- 1/8 tsp. salt

- 1 cup whole milk

- 1 tsp. vanilla extract

- 8 egg whites, at room temperature

Filling

2/3 cup unsalted butter, softened

- 2 1/2 cups powdered sugar

- 1/4 cup light rum

Frosting

2 cups granulated sugar

- 2 egg whites, at room temperature

- 1 cup water

- 1 1/2 tsp. light rum

Directions

1. To make the cake batter, add the butter to a mixing bowl. Using a mixer on medium speed, beat for 30 seconds. With the mixer running, slowly add the granulated sugar. Mix until smooth and combined. Add the cake flour, baking powder, salt, milk, water and vanilla extract. Mix only until well combined and the batter is smooth.

2. In a separate mixing bowl, add the egg whites. Using a mixer on medium speed, beat until stiff peaks form. Gently fold the egg whites into the cake batter. Spray two 9" round cake pans with non stick cooking spray. Spoon the batter into the cake pans.

3. Preheat the oven to 350°. Bake for 35 minutes or until a toothpick inserted in the center of the cakes comes out clean. Remove the cakes from the oven and cool the cakes for 10 minutes in the pans. Remove the cakes from the pans and cool completely before filling and frosting.

4. To make the filling, add the butter, powdered sugar and rum to a mixing bowl. Using a mixer on

medium speed, beat until smooth and combined. Refrigerate the filling until chilled .

5. To make the frosting, add the granulated sugar, egg whites and water to the top of a double boiler over medium heat. Stir until combined. Using a hand mixer on medium speed, beat for 30 seconds. Continue mixing and beat for 7 minutes or until stiff peaks form. The frosting should be hot. Remove the pan from the heat. Add the rum and beat for 2 minutes. The frosting should be firm enough to spread when ready. Do not make the frosting until you are ready to frost the cake.

6. Fill the cake with the filling. Refrigerate the cake until chilled before frosting. Frost the chilled cake and serve. Store the cake in the refrigerator.

Queen Cake

Ingredients

- 1 1/2 cups unsalted butter, softened

- 1 1/2 cups granulated sugar

- 3 eggs

- 2 1/4 cups cake flour

- 2 tsp. baking powder

- 1/2 tsp. salt

- 1/2 cup plus 3 tsp. whole milk

- 1 tsp. vanilla extract

Frosting

- 2 cups granulated sugar

- 2 egg whites

- 1/8 tsp. cream of tartar

- 1/8 tsp. salt

- 1/4 cup plus 2 tbs. water

- 1 tsp. vanilla extract

Directions

1. To make the cake batter, add the butter to a mixing bowl. Using a mixer on medium speed, beat for 30 seconds. With the mixer running, slowly add the granulated sugar. Mix until smooth and combined. Add the eggs and beat for 2 minutes. Add the cake flour, baking powder, salt, milk and vanilla extract. Mix only until well combined and the batter is smooth.

2. Spray three 9" round cake pans with non stick cooking spray. Spoon the batter into the cake pans. Preheat the oven to 350°. Bake for 25 minutes or until a toothpick inserted in the center of the cakes

comes out clean. Remove the cakes from the oven and cool the cakes for 10 minutes in the pans. Remove the cakes from the pans and cool completely before frosting.

3. To make the frosting, add the granulated sugar, egg whites, cream of tartar, salt and water to the top of a double boiler. Stir until combined. Using a hand mixer on medium speed, beat for 7 minutes or until stiff peaks form and the frosting is thick enough to spread. Remove the pan from the heat and stir in the vanilla extract. Cool the frosting for 5 minutes. Spread the frosting between the layers and on the top and sides of the cake.

King Cake

Ingredients

Cake Batter

- 2 cups sour cream
- 1/3 cup plus 1 tbs. granulated sugar
- 1/4 cup unsalted butter, softened
- 1 tsp. salt
- 2 pkgs. active dry yeast
- 1/2 cup warm water
- 2 eggs
- 6 1/2 cups all purpose flour
- 1/2 cup granulated sugar
- 1 1/2 tsp. ground cinnamon
- 1/3 cup unsalted butter, softened

Colored Frostings

- 3 cups powdered sugar
- 3 tbs. melted unsalted butter
- 5 tbs. whole milk
- 1/4 tsp. vanilla extract
- 2 drops liquid green food coloring
- 2 drops liquid yellow food coloring
- 1 drop liquid red food coloring
- 1 drop liquid blue food coloring

Colored Sugars

1 1/2 cups granulated sugar

- 2 drops liquid green food coloring

- 2 drops liquid yellow food coloring

- 1 drop liquid red food coloring

- 1 drop liquid blue food coloring

Directions

1. To make the cake batter, add the sour cream, 1/3 cup granulated sugar, 1/4 cup softened butter and salt to a sauce pan over medium heat. Stir constantly and cook until the butter melts. Remove the pan from the heat and cool the mixture to 110°.

2. In a small bowl, add the yeast, 1 tablespoon granulated sugar and warm water. Stir until the yeast dissolves. Let the yeast sit for 5 minutes. In a large mixing bowl, add the sour cream mixture from the pan, yeast, eggs and 2 cups all purpose flour. Using a mixer on medium speed, beat for 2 minutes. Add 3 cups all purpose flour to the bowl. Mix until combined and a soft dough forms.

3. Lightly flour your work surface. Place the dough on your surface. Knead in 1 1/2 cups all purpose flour. Knead for 10 minutes or until the dough is smooth and elastic .

4. Spray a large bowl with non stick cooking spray. Place the dough in the bowl. Turn the dough so all sides of the dough are coated in the cooking spray. Cover the bowl with a clean dish cloth. Let the dough rise in a warm place for 1 hour or until the dough is doubled in size.

5. In a small bowl, add 1/2 cup granulated sugar and cinnamon. Stir until combined. Punch the dough down and divide the dough into two equal portions. Lightly flour your work surface. Roll each portion into a 27" x 10" rectangle. Spread 1/3 cup softened butter over the dough. Sprinkle the cinnamon sugar over the butter.

6. Starting on a long side, roll the dough up like a jelly roll. Tuck the ends under and pinch the seams and edges closed with your fingers. Spray two large baking sheets with non stick cooking. Place a roll on each baking sheet. Form each roll into an oval shape and pinch the ends together. Let the cakes rise in a warm place for 30 minutes or until they are doubled in bulk.

7. Preheat the oven to 375°. Bake for 20 minutes or until the cakes are lightly browned. Remove the cakes from the oven and cool at least 20 minutes before frosting and decorating.

8. To make the colored frostings, add the powdered sugar, butter, 3 tablespoons milk and vanilla extract to a mixing bowl. Using a mixer on medium speed, beat until light and fluffy. Add the remaining milk if needed to make a creamy and fluffy frosting. Divide the frosting into 3 equal portions and place each portion in a separate bowl. Add the green food coloring to one portion and stir until combined. Add the yellow food coloring to one portion and stir until combined. Add the red and blue food coloring to one portion. Stir until combined and a purple color forms. Spread the coloring frostings on 1/3 of each cake. You can frost the cakes any way you would like. Frosting in the 3 colors is the traditional way. Have fun with the cake and frost any way you like.

9. To make the colored sugars, add 1/2 cup granulated sugar to 3 separate bowls. Add the green food coloring to one bowl, yellow food coloring to one bowl and the red and blue coloring to the final

bowl. Using a fork, stir until well combined and the sugar is brightly colored. Sprinkle the green sugar over the green frosting, red sugar over the red frosting and the purple sugar over the purple frosting on the cake.

Alabama Lane Cake

Ingredients

- 1 cup unsalted butter, softened
- 2 cups granulated sugar
- 3 1/4 cups cake flour
- 2 tsp. baking powder
- 1/8 tsp. salt
- 1 cup whole milk
- 2 tsp. vanilla extract
- 8 egg whites, at room temperature

Filling

- 8 egg yolks, at room temperature
- 1 cup granulated sugar
- 1/2 cup unsalted butter, softened
- 1 cup maraschino cherries, finely chopped
- 1 cup pecans, finely chopped
- 3/4 cup seedless raisins, finely chopped
- 3/4 cup unsweetened grated coconut
- 2 tbs. bourbon

Frosting

- 1/2 cup granulated sugar
- 1/4 cup light corn syrup
- 2 tbs. water
- 1/8 tsp. salt
- 2 egg whites, at room temperature
- 1/2 tsp. vanilla extract

Directions

1. To make the cake batter, add the butter to a mixing bowl. Using a mixer on medium speed, beat for 30 seconds. With the mixer running, slowly add the granulated sugar. Mix until smooth and combined. Add the cake flour, baking powder, salt, milk and vanilla extract. Mix only until well combined and the batter is smooth.

2. In a separate mixing bowl, add the egg whites. Using a mixer on medium speed, beat until stiff peaks form. Gently fold the egg whites into the cake batter. Spray three 9" round cake pans with non stick cooking spray. Spoon the batter into the cake pans.

3. Preheat the oven to 375°. Bake for 20 minutes or until a toothpick inserted in the center of the cakes comes out clean. Remove the cakes from the oven and cool the cakes for 10 minutes in the pans. Remove the cakes from the pans and cool completely before filling and frosting .

4. To make the filling, add the egg yolks, granulated sugar and butter to a sauce pan over medium heat. Stir constantly and cook until the filling thickens and bubbles. Remove the pan from the heat. Add the maraschino cherries, pecans, raisins, coconut and bourbon. Stir until combined. Cool the filling completely before using.

5. To make the frosting, add the granulated sugar, corn syrup, water and salt to a sauce pan over medium heat. Stir constantly and cook until the temperature reaches 242° on a candy thermometer. Remove the pan from the heat.

6. In a mixing bowl, add the egg whites. Using a mixer on medium speed, beat until soft peaks form. While the mixer is running, slowly add the syrup from the pan. Add the vanilla extract and mix until stiff peaks form and the frosting is thick enough to spread. The frosting will be slightly warm when applied to the cake.

7. Place the filling between the layers and frost the top and sides of the cake with the frosting.

Old Fashioned Cajun Wedding Cake

Ingredients

- 1 cup unsalted butter, softened

- 2 cups granulated sugar

- 4 eggs, separated and at room temperature

- 3 cups all purpose flour

- 1 tbs. baking powder

- 1/8 tsp. salt

- 1 cup whole milk

- 1 1/2 tsp. almond extract

Frosting

- 1 1/2 cups granulated sugar

- 2 egg whites, at room temperature

- 1 1/2 tsp. light corn syrup

- 1/4 cup plus 1 tbs. water

- 1/4 tsp. cream of tartar

- 1 cup chopped raisins

- 1 cup chopped pecans

- 1/2 cup sweetened flaked coconut

- 1 tsp. vanilla extract

- 1/2 tsp. almond extract

Directions

1. To make the cake batter, add the butter to a mixing bowl. Using a mixer on medium speed, beat for 30 seconds. With the mixer running, slowly add the granulated sugar. Mix until smooth and combined. Add the eggs and beat for 3 minutes. Add the all purpose flour, baking powder, salt, milk and almond extract. Mix only until well combined and the batter is smooth.

2. Spray two 8" square cake pans with non stick cooking spray. Spoon the batter into the cake pans. Preheat the oven to 350°. Bake for 45 minutes or until a toothpick inserted in the center of the cakes comes out clean. Remove the cakes from the oven and cool the cakes for 10 minutes in the pans. Remove the cakes from the pans and cool completely before frosting.

3. To make the frosting, add the granulated sugar, egg whites, corn syrup, water and cream of tartar to the top of a double boiler. Stir until combined. Using a hand mixer on medium speed, beat for 7 minutes or until stiff peaks form and the frosting is thick enough to spread. Remove the pan from the heat and stir in the raisins, pecans, coconut, vanilla extract and almond extract. Cool the frosting for 5 minutes. Spread the frosting between the layers and on the top and sides of the cake.

Basic Yellow Cake

Ingredients

- 1 cup unsalted butter, softened

- 1 1/2 cups granulated sugar

- 4 eggs

- 3 cups sifted cake flour

- 2 1/2 tsp. baking powder

- 1/2 tsp. salt

- 1 cup whole milk

- 2 tsp. vanilla extract

Directions

1. Preheat the oven to 350°. Spray three 9" round cake pans with non stick cooking spray. In a mixing bowl, add the butter and granulated sugar. Using a mixer on medium speed, beat for 4 minutes. Add the eggs and beat for 3 minutes. Turn the mixer speed to low. Add the cake flour, baking powder, salt, milk and vanilla extract. Mix only until the cake batter is smooth and combined.

2. Spoon the batter into the cake pans. Bake for 20 minutes or until a toothpick inserted in the center of the cakes comes out clean. Remove the cakes from the oven and cool the cakes in the pans for 10 minutes. Remove the cakes from the pans and cool completely before frosting. Frost with your favorite frosting.

Moist and Fluffy White Cake

Ingredients

- 3/4 cup vegetable shortening

- 1 1/2 cups granulated sugar

- 2 1/4 cups sifted cake flour

- 1 tbs. baking powder

- 3/4 tsp. salt

- 1 cup whole milk

- 1 1/2 tsp. clear vanilla extract

- 5 egg whites, at room temperature

Directions

1. Preheat the oven to 350°. Spray two 9" round cake pans with non stick cooking spray. In a mixing bowl, add the vegetable shortening and granulated sugar. Using a mixer on medium speed, beat for 4 minutes. Turn the mixer speed to low. Add the cake flour, baking powder, salt, milk and vanilla extract. Mix only until the cake batter is smooth and combined.

2. In a separate mixing bowl, add the egg whites. Using a mixer on medium speed, beat until stiff peaks form. Fold the egg whites into the cake batter.

3. Spoon the batter into the cake pans. Bake for 25 minutes or until a toothpick inserted in the center of the cakes comes out clean. Remove the cakes from the oven and cool the cakes in the pans for 10 minutes. Remove the cakes from the pans and cool completely before frosting. Frost with your favorite frosting.

Basic Chocolate Cake

Ingredients

- 1/2 cup vegetable shortening

- 2 cups granulated sugar

- 2 eggs, at room temperature

- 4 oz. unsweetened baking chocolate, melted

- 2 1/4 cups sifted cake flour

- 1/2 tsp. baking powder

- 1 tsp. baking soda

- 3/4 tsp. salt

- 3/4 cup buttermilk

- 3/4 cup water

- 1 tsp. vanilla extract

Directions

1. Preheat the oven to 350°. Spray two 9" round cake pans with non stick cooking spray. In a mixing bowl, add the vegetable shortening and granulated sugar. Using a mixer on medium speed, beat for 4 minutes. Add the eggs and beat for 3 minutes. Add the melted chocolate and mix until combined. Turn the mixer speed to low. Add the cake flour, baking powder, baking soda, salt, buttermilk, water and vanilla extract. Mix only until the cake batter is smooth and combined.

2. Spoon the batter into the cake pans. Bake for 30 minutes or until a toothpick inserted in the center of the cakes comes out clean. Remove the cakes from the oven and cool the cakes in the pans for 10 minutes. Remove the cakes from the pans and cool completely before frosting. Frost with your favorite frosting.

Boston Cream Pie

Ingredients

- 1/2 cup unsalted butter, softened

- 1 cup granulated sugar

- 3 eggs

- 2 cups sifted cake flour

- 2 tsp. baking powder

- 1/4 tsp. salt

- 1/2 cup whole milk

- 2 tsp. vanilla extract

- 1/2 tsp. butter flavoring

Cream Filling

- 1/2 cup granulated sugar

- 3 tbs. cornstarch

- 1/4 tsp. salt

- 2 cups whole milk

- 4 egg yolks, beaten

- 1 tsp. vanilla extract

Chocolate Glaze

- 2 tbs. unsalted butter

- 1 oz. unsweetened baking chocolate

- 1 cup powdered sugar

- 2 tbs. boiling water

Directions

1. To make the cake batter, add the butter and granulated sugar to a mixing bowl. Using mixer on medium speed, beat for 3 minutes. Add the eggs and beat for 3 minutes. Add the cake flour, baking powder, salt, milk, vanilla extract and butter flavoring. Mix only until the batter is smooth and combined.

2. Preheat the oven to 350°. Spray two 9" round cake pans with non stick cooking spray. Spoon the batter into the cake pans. Bake for 18 minutes or until a toothpick inserted in the center of the cakes comes out clean. Remove the cakes from the oven. Cool the cakes in the pans for 10 minutes. Remove the cakes from the pans and cool completely before filling and glazing.

3. To make the filling, add the granulated sugar, cornstarch, salt, milk and egg yolks to a sauce pan over medium heat. Stir constantly and cook until the filling thickens and bubbles. Boil for 1 additional minute. Remove the pan from the heat and stir in the vanilla extract. Cool the filling completely before using .

4. To make the glaze, add the butter and chocolate to a small sauce pan over low heat. Stir until the chocolate and butter melt. Remove the pan from the heat and cool for 4 minutes. Add the powdered sugar and boiling water to the pan. Stir until the glaze is smooth and combined.

5. When ready to assemble the cake, place one cake layer on a serving platter. Spread the filling over the cake layer. Place the remaining cake layer on top. Spread the chocolate glaze over the top. Chill the cake at least 2 hours before serving. Store the cake in the refrigerator.

Pineapple Upside Down Cake

Ingredients

- 4 tbs. unsalted butter

- 1/2 cup light brown sugar

- 3 eggs, separated

- 1 cup granulated sugar

- 1 cup self rising flour

- 5 tbs. pineapple juice

- 5 canned pineapple slices

- 5 maraschino cherries

Directions

1. Preheat the oven to 350°. Add the butter and brown sugar to a 10" cast iron skillet. Place the skillet in the oven until the butter and brown sugar sugar melt. In a mixing bowl, add the egg yolks and granulated sugar. Using a mixer on medium speed, beat for 3 minutes. Add the self rising flour and the pineapple juice. Beat for 1 minute or until the batter is well blended.

2. In a separate bowl, add the egg whites. Using a mixer on medium speed, beat until stiff peaks form. Fold the egg whites into the cake batter. Remove the skillet from the oven and stir the butter and brown sugar until combined. Place the pineapple slices in the skillet. Cut the slices if necessary to make them fit. Place a maraschino cherry in the center of each slice. Pour the cake batter over the pineapple slices.

3. Bake for 30 minutes or until a toothpick inserted in the center of the cake comes out clean. Immediately invert the skillet onto a serving platter. Serve hot or cold.

Pineapple Ambrosia Upside Down Cake

Ingredients

- 1/4 cup unsalted butter

- 1/3 cup light brown sugar

- 7 canned pineapple slices

- 7 maraschino cherries

- 12 walnut halves

- 2 1/2 tbs. vegetable shortening

- 2 1/2 tbs. unsalted butter, softened

- 1 tsp. grated orange zest

- 2/3 cup granulated sugar

- 1 egg

- 1 1/4 cups all purpose flour

- 2 tsp. baking powder

- 1/2 tsp. salt

- 1/2 cup whole milk

- 1/3 cup sweetened flaked coconut

- 1 cup whipped cream

Directions

1. Preheat the oven to 350°. Add 1/4 cup butter to a 10" cast iron skillet. Place the skillet in the oven until the butter melts. Remove the skillet from the oven and sprinkle the brown sugar over the butter. Place 7 pineapple slices over the brown sugar. Place a maraschino cherry in the center of each pineapple slice. Place the walnut halves between the pineapple slices.

2. In a mixing bowl, add the vegetable shortening, 2 1/2 tablespoons butter, orange zest and granulated sugar. Using a mixer on medium speed, beat for 3 minutes. Add the egg and beat for 1 minute. Add the all purpose flour, baking powder, salt and milk. Beat until the batter is smooth and combined. Turn the mixer off and stir in the coconut.

3. Pour the cake batter over the pineapple slices. Bake for 40 minutes or until a toothpick inserted in the center of the cake comes out clean. Remove the cake from the oven and cool the cake for 10 minutes in the skillet. Invert the cake onto a serving platter. Spoon a dollop of whipped cream over each serving. Serve the cake warm or at room temperature.

Pecan Upside Down Cake

Makes a 9" round cake

Ingredients

- 3 tbs. melted unsalted butter

- 1 cup light brown sugar

- 3/4 cup plus 1 tbs. boiling water

- 1 cup chopped pecans

- 2 eggs, separated

- 1 cup granulated sugar

- 1 tsp. vanilla extract

- 1 cup all purpose flour

- 1 1/2 tsp. baking powder

- 1/2 tsp. salt

Directions

1. Preheat the oven to 325°. Add the butter, brown sugar and 1 tablespoon boiling water to a 9" round cake pan. Stir until well combined and spread over the bottom of the pan. Sprinkle the pecans over the top.

2. In a mixing bowl, add the egg yolks. Using a mixer on medium speed, beat for 3 minutes. Add the granulated sugar and vanilla extract. Beat for 3 minutes. Add the all purpose flour, baking powder, salt and 3/4 cup boiling water. Mix until well combined.

3. In a separate bowl, add the egg whites. Using a mixer on medium speed, beat until stiff peaks form. Turn the mixer off and fold the egg whites into the cake batter. Spread the batter over the pecans in the pan. Bake for 30 minutes or until a toothpick inserted in the center of the cake comes out clean. Remove the cake from the oven and cool the cake for 10 minutes in the pan. Invert the pan onto a serving platter. Cool the cake for 10 minutes. Serve warm or at room temperature.

Key Lime Cake

Ingredients

- 18 oz. box lemon cake mix

- 4 serving size pkg. instant lemon pudding mix

- 4 eggs

- 1/2 cup water

- 3/4 cup key lime juice

- 1/2 cup vegetable oil

- 2 cups powdered sugar

Directions

1. Preheat the oven to 350°. Spray a 9 x 13 baking pan with non stick cooking spray. In a mixing bowl, add the lemon cake mix, dry lemon pudding mix, eggs, water, 1/2 cup key lime juice and vegetable oil. Using a mixer on medium speed, beat until the cake batter is smooth and combined.

2. Spoon the batter into the prepared pan. Bake for 30 minutes or until a toothpick inserted in the center of the cake comes out clean. Remove the cake from the oven and cool completely before glazing.

3. In a small bowl, add the powdered sugar and 1/4 cup key lime juice. Whisk until combined and pour over the top of the cooled cake.

Blueberry Topped Red Velvet Snack Cake

Ingredients

- 1/2 cup vegetable shortening

- 2 1/4 cups granulated sugar

- 2 eggs

- 1/4 cup red food coloring

- 1 tsp. white vinegar

- 1 tsp. vanilla extract

- 2 1/4 cups cake flour

- 2 tbs. unsweetened baking cocoa

- 1 tsp. salt

- 1 tsp. baking soda

- 1 cup buttermilk

- 2 tbs. cornstarch

- 1 cup orange juice

- 2 cups fresh blueberries

- 1/8 tsp. ground nutmeg

- 8 oz. carton thawed Cool whip, optional

Directions

1. Preheat the oven to 350°. Spray a 9 x 13 baking pan with non stick cooking spray. In a mixing bowl, add the vegetable shortening and 1 1/2 cups granulated sugar. Using a mixer on medium speed, beat for 4 minutes. Add the eggs and beat until the batter is smooth and combined.

2. Add the red food coloring, white vinegar and vanilla extract to the bowl. Mix until combined. Add the cake flour, baking cocoa, salt, baking soda and buttermilk. Mix only until combined. Spread the batter in the prepared pan.

3. Bake for 30 minutes or until a toothpick inserted in the center of the cake comes out clean. Remove the cake from the oven and cool completely before topping.

4. In a sauce pan over medium heat, add 3/4 cup granulated sugar, cornstarch, orange juice, blueberries and nutmeg. Stir constantly and cook until the topping thickens and bubbles. Reduce the heat to low and cook for 2 minutes. Remove the pan from the heat and cool completely before serving.

5. When ready to serve, spoon the blueberry topping over slices of the cake. Spoon a dollop of Cool Whip over each serving.

Honey Bun Cake

Ingredients

- 18 oz. box yellow cake mix
- 4 eggs
- 2/3 cup vegetable oil
- 1/3 cup water
- 1 cup sour cream
- 1/2 cup light brown sugar
- 1 tsp. ground cinnamon
- 2/3 cup chopped pecans
- 1 cup powdered sugar
- 1 tbs. plus 1 tsp. whole milk
- 1/2 tsp. vanilla extract

Directions

1. Preheat the oven to 350°. Spray a 9 x 13 baking pan with non stick cooking spray. In a mixing bowl, add the yellow cake mix, eggs, vegetable oil, water and sour cream. Using a mixer on medium speed, beat for 3 minutes or until the cake batter is smooth and combined.

2. Pour half the batter into the prepared pan. In a small bowl, add the brown sugar, cinnamon and pecans. Stir until combined and sprinkle half the brown sugar mixture over the batter. Spread the remaining batter in the pan. Sprinkle the remaining brown sugar mixture over the batter.

3. Bake for 30 minutes or until a toothpick inserted in the center of the cake comes out clean. Remove the cake from the oven and let the cake cool while you make the glaze.

4. In a small bowl, add the powdered sugar, milk and vanilla extract. Whisk until combined and pour over the warm cake. Cool the cake completely before serving.

Carrot Sheet Cake

Ingredients

- 1 1/2 cups all purpose flour
- 1 tsp. baking powder
- 1 tsp. baking soda
- 1/2 tsp. salt
- 1 tsp. ground cinnamon
- 1 cup granulated sugar

- 1 1/4 cups grated carrot

- 2/3 cup vegetable oil

- 2 eggs

- 8 oz. can crushed pineapple, drained

- 1 1/2 tsp. vanilla extract

- 3 oz. cream cheese, softened

- 1/4 cup unsalted butter, softened

- 2 1/4 cups powdered sugar

Directions

1. Preheat the oven to 350°. Spray a 9 x 13 baking pan with non stick cooking spray. In a mixing bowl, add the all purpose flour, baking powder, baking soda, salt, cinnamon and granulated sugar. Stir until combined.

2. In a separate mixing bowl, add the carrots, vegetable oil, eggs, pineapple and 1 teaspoon vanilla extract. Using a mixer on medium speed, beat for 3 minutes. Turn the mixer speed to low and add the dry **Ingredients**. Mix only until the cake batter is smooth and combined.

3. Spoon the batter into the prepared pan. Bake for 35 minutes or until a toothpick inserted in the center of the cake comes out clean. Remove the cake from the oven and cool the cake completely before frosting.

4. In a mixing bowl, add the cream cheese, butter and 1/2 teaspoon vanilla extract. Using a mixer on medium speed, beat until smooth and fluffy. Add the powdered sugar to the bowl. Beat until the frosting is light and spreadable. Frost the cake and serve.

Coca Cola Cake

Ingredients

- 2 cups all purpose flour

- 2 cups granulated sugar

- 1 cup unsalted butter, softened

- 3 tbs. unsweetened baking cocoa

- 1 cup Coca Cola

- 1/2 cup whole milk

- 2 eggs, beaten

- 1 tsp. baking soda

- 1 tsp. vanilla extract

- 1 1/2 cups miniature marshmallows

- Frosting recipe below

Directions

1. Preheat the oven to 350°. Spray a 9 x 13 baking pan with non stick cooking spray. Add the all purpose flour and granulated sugar to a large mixing bowl. Stir until combined.

2. In a small saucepan over medium heat, add the butter, baking cocoa and Coca Cola. Stir constantly and bring the mixture to a boil. Remove the pan from the heat and pour over the dry **Ingredients**. Add the whole milk, eggs, baking soda, vanilla extract and marshmallows. Whisk quickly and mix until combined.

3. Pour the batter into the prepared pan. Bake for 25 minutes or until a toothpick inserted in the center of the cake comes out clean. Remove the cake from the oven and cool completely before frosting.

4. Coca Cola Frosting: In a mixing bowl, add 1/2 cup softened butter, 4 cups powdered sugar and 6 tablespoons Coca Cola. Using a mixer on medium speed, beat until light and fluffy. If the frosting is too stiff, add another tablespoon Coca Cola. Spread the frosting on the cooled cake and top with 1/2 cup chopped pecans if desired.

Chocolate Caramel Nut Cake

Ingredients

- 18 oz. box German chocolate cake mix

- 14 oz. pkg. caramels, unwrapped

- 1/2 cup unsalted butter

- 1/3 cup whole milk

- 1 cup chopped dry roasted peanuts

- 3/4 cup milk chocolate chips

Directions

1. Preheat the oven to 350°. Spray a 9 x 13 baking pan with non stick cooking spray. Prepare the cake batter according to package **Directions**. Spread half the batter in the cake pan. Bake for 10 minutes. The cake will not be done at this point. Remove the cake from the oven.

2. In a sauce pan over medium heat, add the caramels, butter and milk. Stir constantly and cook until the caramels and butter melt. Remove the pan from the heat and spread over the partially baked cake in the pan.

3. Sprinkle the peanuts and milk chocolate chips over the caramel. Spread the remaining cake batter over the top. Bake for 20 minutes or until a toothpick inserted in the center of the cake comes out clean. Remove the cake from the oven and cool completely before serving.

Chocolate Sauce Cake

Ingredients

- 1 cup granulated sugar
- 3 tbs. unsweetened baking cocoa
- 1 1/2 cups boiling water
- 2 tbs. unsalted butter, softened
- 1 tsp. vanilla extract
- 1 cup all purpose flour
- 2 tsp. baking powder
- 1/2 tsp. salt
- 1/2 cup whole milk
- 2 cups vanilla ice cream
- 5 maraschino cherries

Directions

1. In a sauce pan over medium heat, add 1/2 cup granulated sugar, 1 tablespoon baking cocoa and the boiling water. Stir constantly and cook for 5 minutes. Remove the pan from the heat.

2. In a mixing bowl, add the butter, vanilla extract and 1/2 cup granulated sugar. Using a mixer on medium speed, beat until smooth and combined. Add the all purpose flour, 2 tablespoons baking cocoa, baking powder, salt and milk. Mix until the cake batter is combined.

3. Spray a 1 1/2 quart casserole dish with non stick cooking spray. Spread the chocolate sauce in the pan over the bottom of the casserole dish. Drop the cake batter, by teaspoonfuls, onto the sauce.

4. Preheat the oven to 375°. Bake for 25 minutes or until a toothpick inserted in the center of the cake comes out clean. Remove the cake from the oven and cool for 15 minutes.

5. Spoon the cake into serving bowls. Place scoops of vanilla ice cream over the cake. Press a maraschino cherry into the ice cream and serve.

Chocolate Cream Cheese Filled Cupcakes

Ingredients

- 18 oz. box devil's food cake mix
- 8 oz. cream cheese, softened
- 1/3 cup granulated sugar

- 1 egg
- 1 cup semisweet chocolate chips

Directions

1. Line your muffin tins with cupcake liners. Preheat the oven to 350°. Prepare the German chocolate cake mix according to the package **Directions**. Spoon the batter into the cupcake liners filling them about 2/3 full.

2. In a mixing bowl, add the cream cheese, granulated sugar and egg. Using a mixer on medium speed, beat until smooth and creamy. Turn the mixer off and stir in the semisweet chocolate chips.

3. Spoon 1 teaspoon cream cheese filling over the center of each cupcake. The filling will drop into the cake batter on its own. Do not push the filling into the cake batter. Bake for 20 minutes or until a toothpick inserted in the center of the cupcakes comes out clean. Remove the cupcakes from the oven. Remove the cupcakes from the muffin tin and cool completely before serving.

Chocolate Filled Cupcakes

Ingredients

- 8 oz. cream cheese, softened
- 1/3 cup granulated sugar
- 1 egg
- 1/8 tsp. salt
- 1 cup sweetened flaked coconut
- 1 cup finely chopped walnuts
- 1 cup miniature semisweet chocolate chips

Cake Batter

- 2 cups granulated sugar
- 1 1/2 cups water
- 3/4 cup vegetable oil
- 2 eggs
- 2 tsp. vanilla extract
- 1 tsp. white vinegar
- 3 cups all purpose flour
- 1/2 cup unsweetened baking cocoa

- 1 tsp. baking soda

- 1 tsp. salt

Frosting

- 1 1/3 cups semisweet chocolate chips

- 1/2 heavy whipping cream

Directions

1. To make the filling, add the cream cheese and granulated sugar to a mixing bowl. Using a mixer on medium speed, beat until light and fluffy. Add the egg and salt. Mix until combined. Turn the mixer off and stir in the coconut, walnuts and chocolate chips.

2. To make the cake batter, add the granulated sugar, water, vegetable oil, eggs, vanilla extract and white vinegar to a mixing bowl. Using a mixer on medium speed, beat for 4 minutes. Add the all purpose flour, baking cocoa, baking soda and salt to the bowl. Mix only until combined.

3. Preheat the oven to 350°. Place cupcake liners in your miniature muffin tins. Spoon the cake batter into the muffin cups filling them about 1/3 full. Spoon 1 teaspoon filling into the cake batter. Spoon enough cake batter over the filling to fill the muffin cups 3/4 full.

4. Bake for 12 minutes or until a toothpick inserted in the center of the cupcakes comes out clean. Remove the cupcakes from the oven and cool the cupcakes in the pan for 10 minutes. Remove the cupcakes from the pan and cool completely before frosting .

5. To make the frosting, add the chocolate chips and heavy whipping cream to a sauce pan over low heat. Stir constantly and cook until the chocolate chips melt. Remove the pan from the heat and cool completely at room temperature. Whip the frosting until smooth. Frost the cupcakes and serve.

Homemade Chocolate Cupcakes

Ingredients

- 1/2 cup unsalted butter, softened

- 1 cup granulated sugar

- 1 egg

- 1 tsp. vanilla extract

- 1 1/2 cups all purpose flour

- 1/2 cup unsweetened baking cocoa

- 1 tsp. baking soda

- 1/4 tsp. salt

- 1/2 cup water

- 1/2 cup buttermilk

Directions

1. Preheat the oven to 375°. In a mixing bowl, add the butter and granulated sugar. Using a mixer on medium speed, beat until light and fluffy. Add the egg and vanilla extract to the bowl. Beat until smooth and combined. Add the all purpose flour, baking cocoa, baking soda, salt, water and buttermilk. Mix until the batter is smooth and combined.

2. Line your muffin tin with cupcake liners. Spoon the batter into the muffin cups filling them about 2/3 full. Bake for 12 minutes or until a toothpick inserted in the center of the cupcakes comes out clean. Remove the cupcakes from the oven. Cool the cupcakes for 10 minutes in the pan. Remove the cupcakes from the pan and cool completely before frosting. Frost with your favorite frosting.

Red Velvet Cream Filled Cupcakes

Ingredients

- 2 cups granulated sugar

- 2 cups plus 3 tbs. all purpose flour

- 1/2 cup whole milk

- 1/2 cup plus 1/3 cup vegetable shortening

- 2 eggs

- 1 oz. red food coloring

- 1 tbs. white vinegar

- 2 tsp. vanilla extract

- 3 tbs. unsweetened cocoa

- 1 tsp. baking soda

- 1 cup buttermilk

- 1/2 cup softened unsalted butter

- 1 1/2 cups plus 3 tbs. powdered sugar

- 1 cup semisweet chocolate chips

- 1/3 cup plus 3 tsp. evaporated milk

Directions

1. In a sauce pan over medium heat, add 1/2 cup granulated sugar, 3 tablespoons all purpose flour and milk. Stir constantly and bring the mixture to a boil. Boil for 2 minutes or until the mixture thickens. Remove the pan from the heat and cool completely before using.

2. In a mixing bowl, add 1/2 cup vegetable shortening and 1 1/2 cups granulated sugar. Using a mixer on medium speed, beat until light and fluffy. Add the eggs and mix until well blended. Add the red food coloring, white vinegar and 1 teaspoon vanilla extract. Mix until well combined. Add 2 cups all

purpose flour, cocoa, baking soda and buttermilk. Mix until well combined and the batter is smooth.

3. Preheat the oven to 350°. Line a 24 count muffin tin with cupcake liners. Spoon the cake batter into the muffin cups filling them about 2/3 full. Bake for 20 minutes or until a toothpick inserted in the center of the cupcakes comes out clean. Remove the cupcakes from the oven and cool for 10 minutes in the pan. Remove the cupcakes from the pan and cool completely.

4. In a mixing bowl, add the butter and 1/3 cup vegetable shortening. Using a mixer on medium speed, beat until light and fluffy. Add 3 tablespoons powdered sugar and cooled sugar mixture. Mix until well combined. Spoon the filling into a large pastry bag with a large round tip. Insert the tip halfway in the cupcakes and squeeze until a small amount of filling enters the cupcakes.

5. In a sauce pan over low heat, add the chocolate chips and 1/3 cup evaporated milk. Stir constantly and cook until the chocolate chips melt. Remove the pan from the heat and stir until smooth. Add 1 1/2 cups powdered sugar and 1 teaspoon evaporated milk. Stir until the frosting is smooth and spreadable. Add the remaining evaporated milk if needed to make a spreadable frosting. Frost the cupcakes and serve.

Easy Mix Cupcakes

Ingredients

- 1/2 cup vegetable shortening

- 1 cup granulated sugar

- 2 cups sifted cake flour

- 2 1/4 tsp. baking powder

- 1/2 tsp. salt

- 3 egg yolks, beaten

- 3/4 cup whole milk

- 1 tsp. vanilla extract

Directions

1. Line your muffin tins with cupcake liners. Preheat the oven to 375°. In a mixing bowl, add the vegetable shortening and granulated sugar. Using a mixer on medium speed, beat for 3 minutes. In a separate bowl, add the cake flour, baking powder and salt. Mix until well combined.

2. Add the egg yolks, milk and vanilla extract to the mixing bowl. Mix for 3 minutes. Add the dry **Ingredients** and mix only until combined. Spoon the batter into the cupcake liners filling them about 2/3 full. Bake for 20 minutes or until a toothpick inserted in the cupcakes comes out clean. Remove the cupcakes from the oven. Cool the cupcakes in the muffin tins for 10 minutes. Remove the cupcakes from the muffin tins and cool completely before frosting. Frost with your favorite frosting.

Orange Cupcakes

Ingredients

- 1/2 cup vegetable shortening

- 1 1/2 cups granulated sugar

- 2 eggs

- 1 tsp. baking soda

- 2/3 cup buttermilk

- 2 cups all purpose flour

- 1/2 tsp. salt

- 1 cup chopped pecans

- 1 1/2 tsp. grated orange zest

- 1/2 cup orange juice

Directions

1. Line your muffin tins with cupcake liners. Preheat the oven to 375°. In a mixing bowl, add the vegetable shortening and 1 cup granulated sugar. Using a mixer on medium speed, beat for 3 minutes. Add the eggs and mix for 3 minutes. In a small bowl, add the baking soda and buttermilk. Stir until the baking soda dissolves. Add the all purpose flour, salt and buttermilk to the mixing bowl. Mix until well combined. Turn the mixer off and stir in the pecans.

2. Spoon the batter into the cupcake liners filling them about 2/3 full. Bake for 12 minutes or until a toothpick inserted in the cupcakes comes out clean. Remove the cupcakes from the oven. Cool the cupcakes in the pan while you make the glaze.

3. In a sauce pan over medium heat, add 1/2 cup granulated sugar, orange zest and orange juice. Stir constantly and cook until the syrup comes to a boil. Remove the pan from the heat and cool for 5 minutes. Spoon the syrup over the top of the cupcakes. Leave the cupcakes in the pan until completely cool.

Delicate Cupcakes with Vanilla Buttercream

Ingredients

- 3/4 cup plus 1 1/2 tsp. unsalted butter, softened

- 1 cup granulated sugar

- 2 eggs

- 2 cups all purpose flour

- 2 tsp. baking powder

- 1/4 tsp. salt

- 2/3 cup plus 1 1/2 tbs. whole milk

- 2 1/2 tsp. vanilla extract

- 2 1/4 cups powdered sugar

Directions

1. Line your muffin tins with cupcake liners. Preheat the oven to 375°. In a mixing bowl, add 1/2 cup butter and the granulated sugar. Using a mixer on medium speed, beat for 3 minutes. Add the eggs and mix for 3 minutes. Add the all purpose flour, baking powder, salt, 2/3 cup milk and 1 teaspoon vanilla extract to the mixing bowl. Mix until well combined.

2. Spoon the batter into the cupcake liners filling them about 2/3 full. Bake for 18 minutes or until a toothpick inserted in the cupcakes comes out clean. Remove the cupcakes from the oven. Cool the cupcakes in the muffin tins for 10 minutes. Remove the cupcakes from the muffin tins and cool completely before frosting.

3. In a mixing bowl, add 1/4 cup plus 1 1/2 teaspoons butter, powdered sugar, 1 1/2 tablespoons milk and 1 1/2 teaspoons vanilla extract. Using a mixer on medium speed, beat for 5 minutes. The frosting should be smooth and spreadable when ready. Spread the frosting on the cupcakes and serve.

Banana Sour Cream Cake

Ingredients

- 18 oz. box yellow cake mix

- 1 cup ripe bananas, mashed

- 1/4 cup vegetable oil

- 3 eggs

- 1 cup sour cream

- 8 oz. pkg. cream cheese, softened

- 1/2 cup unsalted butter, softened

- 4 cups powdered sugar

- 1 cup chopped walnuts

Directions

1. Preheat the oven to 350°. Spray a 9 x 13 baking pan with non stick cooking spray. In a large bowl, add the cake mix, bananas, vegetable oil, eggs and sour cream. Using a mixer on medium speed, beat for 3 minutes. The batter should be well combined and smooth with the exception of the banana pieces. Bake for 25 minutes or until a toothpick inserted in the center of the cake comes out clean. Remove the cake from the oven and cool for 4 hours before frosting.

2. In a mixing bowl, add the cream cheese and butter. With a mixer on medium speed, beat for 4 minutes. The cream cheese and butter should be fluffy and well combined. Add the powdered sugar and beat for 4 minutes or until the frosting is thick and spreadable.

3. When the cake has cooled, turn the cake onto a platter. Cut the cake in half cross wise. You should have two equal pieces. Place one half on a serving plate. Top the cake with about 3/4 cup frosting. Place the other cake half on top. Frost the top and sides of the cake with the remaining frosting. Press the walnuts into the sides of the cake for decoration.

4. Store the cake in the refrigerator.

Banana Pineapple Cake

Ingredients

- 1 1/2 cups all purpose flour

- 1 tsp. baking powder

- 1 tsp. baking soda

- 1/2 tsp. salt

- 1 tsp. ground cinnamon

- 1 cup granulated sugar

- 1 1/4 cups mashed banana

- 1/2 cup vegetable oil

- 2 eggs

- 8 oz. can crushed pineapple, drained

- 1 1/2 tsp. vanilla extract

- 3 oz. cream cheese, softened

- 1/4 cup unsalted butter, softened

- 2 1/4 cups powdered sugar

Directions

1. Preheat the oven to 350°. Spray a 9 x 13 baking pan with non stick cooking spray. In a mixing bowl, add the all purpose flour, baking powder, baking soda, salt, cinnamon and granulated sugar. Stir until combined.

2. In a separate mixing bowl, add the banana, vegetable oil, eggs, pineapple and 1 teaspoon vanilla extract. Using a mixer on medium speed, beat for 3 minutes. Turn the mixer speed to low and add the dry **Ingredients**. Mix only until the cake batter is smooth and combined.

3. Spoon the batter into the prepared pan. Bake for 35 minutes or until a toothpick inserted in the center of the cake comes out clean. Remove the cake from the oven and cool the cake completely before frosting.

4. In a mixing bowl, add the cream cheese, butter and 1/2 teaspoon vanilla extract. Using a mixer on medium speed, beat until smooth and fluffy. Add the powdered sugar to the bowl. Beat until the frosting is light and spreadable. Frost the cake and serve.

Mississippi Mud Cake

Ingredients

- 1 cup unsalted butter

- 2 cups granulated sugar

- 4 eggs, lightly beaten

- 1 tsp. vanilla extract

- 1 1/2 cups all purpose flour

- 1/2 cup unsweetened cocoa

- 1/8 tsp. salt

- 1 1/2 cups chopped pecans

- 1 1/2 cups miniature marshmallows

- Chocolate Frosting below

Directions

1. Preheat the oven to 350°. Spray a 9 x 13 baking pan with non stick cooking spray. In a large saucepan, add the butter and granulated sugar. Stir until the granulated sugar and butter melt. Do not use a mixer for this recipe. Remove the pan from the heat and whisk in the beaten eggs and vanilla extract.

2. Add the all purpose flour, unsweetened cocoa, salt and 1 cup chopped pecans. Stir until the batter is well combined. Spread the batter into the prepared pan. Bake for 15 minutes or until a toothpick inserted in the center of the cakes comes out clean. You do not want to over bake this batter. It is a dense batter similar to fudge brownies.

3. Remove the cake from the oven and immediately sprinkle the marshmallows over the cake. The heat from the cake will soften the marshmallows.

4. While the cake is still warm, pour the chocolate frosting all over the cake. Using the back of a spoon, make sure the frosting completely covers the cake including the corners. Sprinkle 1/2 cup pecans over the top of the frosting. Let the cake cool completely before serving.

5. Chocolate Frosting: In a mixing bowl, add 4 cups powdered sugar, 1/2 cup whole milk, 1/3 cup unsweetened cocoa and 1/4 cup melted unsalted butter. Mix with a whisk until well combined. Pour over the warm cake.

Peanut Butter Sheet Cake

Ingredients

- 3/4 cup unsalted butter, softened

- 3/4 cup creamy peanut butter

- 2 cups light brown sugar

- 3 eggs

- 2 cups all purpose flour

- 1 tbs. baking powder

- 1/2 tsp. salt

- 1 cup whole milk

- 1 tsp. vanilla extract

Directions

1. Preheat the oven to 350°. Spray a 9 x 13 baking pan with non stick cooking spray. In a mixing bowl, add the butter, peanut butter and brown sugar. Using a mixer on medium speed, beat for 3 minutes. Add the eggs and beat for 2 minutes. Add the all purpose flour, baking powder, salt, milk and vanilla extract. Mix only until the cake batter is smooth and combined.

2. Spoon the cake batter into the prepared pan. Bake for 45 minutes or until a toothpick inserted in the center of the cake comes out clean. Remove the cake from the oven and cool completely before frosting.

3. Chocolate, peanut butter, vanilla and cream cheese frosting are all delicious on this cake. My family prefers chocolate frosting and topped with finely chopped peanuts.

Pineapple Nut Cake

Ingredients

- 2 cups all purpose flour

- 2 cups granulated sugar

- 2 eggs

- 2 tsp. baking soda

- 1/2 tsp. salt

- 1 cup chopped pecans

- 20 oz. can crushed pineapple, drained

- 8 oz. cream cheese, softened

- 1/2 cup unsalted butter, softened

- 2 tbs. whole milk

- 2 cups powdered sugar

- 1 tsp. vanilla extract

Directions

1. Preheat the oven to 350°. Spray a 9 x 13 baking pan with non stick cooking spray. In a mixing bowl, add the all purpose flour, granulated sugar, eggs, baking soda, salt, pecans and crushed pineapple. Using a mixer on low speed, beat until well combined. Pour the batter into the prepared pan.

2. Bake for 35 minutes or until a toothpick inserted in the center of the cake comes out clean. Remove the cake from the oven and cool for 30 minutes before frosting.

3. In a mixing bowl, add the cream cheese and butter. Using a mixer on medium speed, beat until smooth and combined. Add the milk, powdered sugar and vanilla extract to the bowl. Mix until smooth and creamy. Spread the frosting on a slightly warm cake. Store the cake in the refrigerator.

Apple Honey Upside Down Cake

Ingredients

- 1/2 cup plus 2 tbs. unsalted butter, softened

- 1/2 cup light brown sugar

- 1 large apple, peeled and cored

- 4 maraschino cherries, halved

- 3/4 cup honey

- 1 beaten egg

- 1/4 tsp. baking soda

- 1/2 cup buttermilk

- 1 1/2 cups all purpose flour

- 1 tsp. baking powder

- 1 tsp. pumpkin pie spice

Directions

1. Preheat the oven to 350°. Add 2 tablespoons butter to a 9" cast iron skillet. Place the skillet in the oven until the butter melts. Remove the skillet from the oven. Sprinkle the brown sugar over the melted butter.

2. Slice the apple into 8 thin rings and place the rings in the skillet. The apple rings may overlap. Place a maraschino cherry half in the center of each apple ring.

3. In a mixing bowl, add 1/2 cup butter and honey. Using a mixer on medium speed, beat until smooth and combined. Add the egg and beat until combined. In a small bowl, add the baking soda and buttermilk. Stir until the baking soda dissolves and add to the bowl. Add the all purpose flour, baking powder and pumpkin pie spice. Mix until the batter is smooth and combined.

4. Pour the batter over the apples in the skillet. Bake for 45 minutes or until a toothpick inserted in the center of the cake comes out clean. Remove the cake from the oven and cool the cake in the skillet for 5 minutes. Invert the cake onto a serving platter. Cool for 10 minutes before serving. Serve the cake warm or at room temperature.

Apple Upside Down Cake

Ingredients

- 1 1/2 tbs. unsalted butter

- 3/4 cup light brown sugar

- 1 1/2 tsp. ground cinnamon

- 3 apples, peeled, cored and cut into rings

- 1/4 cup vegetable shortening

- 1/2 cup molasses

- 1 egg

- 1 1/4 cups all purpose flour

- 3/4 tsp. baking soda

- 1/4 tsp. salt

- 3/4 tsp. ground ginger

- 1/2 cup buttermilk

- 1 cup whipped cream

Directions

1. Preheat the oven to 350°. Add the butter to a 9" cast iron skillet. Place the skillet in the oven until the butter melts. Remove the skillet from the oven. In a small bowl, stir together 1/2 cup brown sugar and 1 teaspoon cinnamon. Sprinkle the brown sugar over the melted butter. Place the apple rings in the skillet over the brown sugar. The apple rings may overlap.

2. In a mixing bowl, add the vegetable shortening and 1/4 cup brown sugar. Using a mixer on medium speed, beat until smooth and combined. Add the molasses and egg to the bowl. Beat until combined. Add the all purpose flour, baking soda, salt, ginger and buttermilk. Mix until the batter is smooth and combined.

3. Pour the batter over the apples in the skillet. Bake for 45 minutes or until a toothpick inserted in the center of the cake comes out clean. Remove the cake from the oven and cool the cake in the skillet for 5 minutes. Invert the cake onto a serving platter. Cool for 10 minutes before serving. Spoon a dollop of whipped cream over each serving. Serve the cake warm or at room temperature.

Cherry Upside Down Cake

Ingredients

- 1/2 cup light brown sugar

- 16 oz. can tart cherries

- 1/3 cup vegetable shortening

- 1 1/2 cups granulated sugar

- 1 egg

- 1 3/4 cups all purpose flour

- 1 tsp. baking powder

- 1/2 tsp. salt

- 1 cup evaporated milk

- 1 tsp. vanilla extract

- 1 1/2 tbs. cornstarch

- 1/8 tsp. almond extract

- 1 drop red food coloring

Directions

1. Preheat the oven to 350°. Spray a 9 x 13 baking pan with non stick cooking spray. Sprinkle the brown sugar over the bottom of the pan. Drain the cherries but reserve the juice. You need 1 1/2 cups juice for this recipe. Add water to make 1 1/2 cups reserved juice if needed.

2. Spoon the cherries over the brown sugar. In a mixing bowl, add the vegetable shortening and 1 cup granulated sugar. Using a mixer on medium speed, beat until smooth and combined. Add the egg and beat until combined. Add the all purpose flour, baking powder, salt, evaporated milk and vanilla extract. Mix until the batter is smooth and combined.

3. Pour the batter over the cherries in the pan. Bake for 40 minutes or until a toothpick inserted in the center of the cake comes out clean. Remove the cake from the oven. Cool the cake while you prepare the sauce.

4. In a sauce pan over medium heat, add the 1 1/2 cups reserved cherry juice, 1/2 cup granulated sugar and cornstarch. Stir constantly and cook until the mixture thickens and bubbles. Remove the pan from the heat and stir in the almond extract and red food coloring. Refrigerate the sauce until cool. Spoon the sauce over the cake and serve.

Toasted Coconut Cake

Ingredients

- 3/4 cup unsalted butter, softened
- 2 cups granulated sugar
- 4 eggs, separated and at room temperature
- 2 1/2 cups all purpose flour
- 1 tbs. baking powder
- 1/2 tsp. salt
- 1 tsp. vanilla extract
- 1 cup light brown sugar
- 3/4 cup half and half
- 2 cups sweetened flaked coconut

Directions

1. Preheat the oven to 350°. Spray a 9 x 13 baking pan with non stick cooking spray. In a mixing bowl, add 1/2 cup butter and granulated sugar. Using a mixer on medium speed, beat for 3 minutes. Add the egg yolks and beat for 3 minutes. Add the all purpose flour, baking powder, salt and vanilla extract. Beat until the batter is smooth and combined.

2. In a separate mixing bowl, add the egg whites. Using a mixer on medium speed, beat until stiff peaks form. Gently fold the egg whites into the cake batter. Spread the batter into the prepared pan. Bake for 50 minutes or until a toothpick inserted in the center of the cake comes out clean. Remove the cake from the oven and let the cake cool while you prepare the topping.

3. In a mixing bowl, add 1/4 cup butter, brown sugar, half and half and coconut. Stir until well combined. Spread the topping over the top of the cake. Turn the oven to the broiler position. Broil for 3 minutes or until the topping is golden brown. Remove the cake from the oven and cool completely before serving.

Fruit Cocktail Cake

Ingredients

- 3 cups granulated sugar
- 2 cups all purpose flour
- 1 tsp. baking soda
- 1/8 tsp. salt
- 16 oz. can fruit cocktail

- 5 oz. can evaporated milk

- 1/2 cup unsalted butter

- 1/2 cup chopped pecans

Directions

1. Preheat the oven to 350°. Spray a 9 x 13 baking pan with non stick cooking spray. In a mixing bowl, add 2 cups granulated sugar, all purpose flour, baking soda and salt. Stir until combined. Add the fruit cocktail with juice to the dry **Ingredients**. Whisk until the batter is well combined. Spread the batter into the prepared pan.

2. Bake for 45 minutes or until a toothpick inserted in the center of the cake comes out clean. Remove the cake from the oven. While the cake is baking, make the topping.

3. In a sauce pan over medium heat, add the evaporated milk, 1 cup granulated sugar and butter. Stir constantly and cook about 10 minutes or until the topping thickens and bubbles. Remove the pan from the heat and stir in the pecans.

4. Spread the topping over the hot cake. Cool the cake completely before serving.

Oatmeal Cake

Ingredients

- 1 1/4 cups boiling water

- 1 cup old fashioned oats

- 1/2 cup plus 6 tbs. unsalted butter, softened

- 1 1/2 cups granulated sugar

- 1 cup light brown sugar

- 2 eggs

- 1 1/2 cups all purpose flour

- 1 tsp. baking soda

- 1/2 tsp. ground cinnamon

- 1/4 tsp. salt

- 1 cup chopped pecans

- 1 cup sweetened flaked coconut

- 1/4 cup heavy whipping cream

- 2 tsp. vanilla extract

Directions

1. In a mixing bowl, add the boiling water and oats. Let the oats sit for 20 minutes at room temperature. Add 1/2 cup butter, 1 cup granulated sugar, brown sugar, eggs, all purpose flour, baking soda, cinnamon and salt to the oats. Whisk until well combined.

2. Preheat the oven to 300°. Spray a 9 x 13 baking pan with non stick cooking spray. Spoon the batter into the pan. Bake for 45 minutes or until a toothpick inserted in the center of the cake comes out clean. Remove the cake from the oven and cool the cake slightly while you make the frosting.

3. In a mixing bowl, add the pecans, coconut, 1/2 cup granulated sugar, heavy whipping cream, 6 tablespoons butter and vanilla extract. Stir until combined and spread over the warm cake. Turn the oven to the broiler position. Broil the cake for 4 minutes or until the topping is golden brown. Remove the cake from the oven and cool for 10 minutes before serving. Serve the cake warm or at room temperature.

Oatmeal Spice Cake

Ingredients

- 1/2 cup quick cooking oats

- 1/3 cup boiling water

- 3/4 cup evaporated milk

- 1/2 cup vegetable shortening

- 1/4 cup granulated sugar

- 1 cup light brown sugar

- 2 eggs

- 1 1/4 cups all purpose flour

- 1/2 tsp. baking soda

- 1/2 tsp. salt

- 1/2 tsp. ground cinnamon

- 1/2 tsp. ground cloves

- 1/2 cup raisins

- 1/2 cup chopped pecans

Directions

1. In a small bowl, add the oats, boiling water and evaporated milk. Set the oats aside for now. Add the vegetable shortening, granulated sugar and brown sugar to a mixing bowl. Using a mixer on medium speed, beat for 2 minutes. Add 1 cup all purpose flour, baking soda, salt, cinnamon, cloves and the oats. Mix until well combined. Turn the mixer off.

2. In a small bowl, add 1/4 cup all purpose flour, raisins and pecans. Toss until the raisins and pecans

are coated in the all purpose flour. Add the raisins and pecans to the cake batter. Stir until combined.

3. Preheat the oven to 350°. Spray a 9" square baking pan with non stick cooking spray. Spoon the batter into the pan. Bake for 45 minutes or until a toothpick inserted in the center of the cake comes out clean. Remove the cake from the oven and cool completely before serving.

Lemon Delight Cake

Ingredients

- 18 oz. box lemon cake mix
- 1 1/3 cups water
- 3 eggs
- 1/3 cup unsweetened applesauce
- 8 oz. cream cheese, softened
- 1 cup powdered sugar
- 15 oz. can lemon pie filling
- 1/3 cup light brown sugar
- 1/4 cup chopped pecans
- 3 tbs. all purpose flour
- 4 1/2 tsp. melted unsalted butter
- 1/2 tsp. ground cinnamon
- 1/8 tsp. vanilla extract
- 4 tsp. lemon juice

Directions

1. In a mixing bowl, add the cake mix, water, eggs and applesauce. Using a mixer on medium speed, beat until well combined. Spray a 9 x 13 baking pan with non stick cooking spray. Spread half the batter into the pan.

2. In a mixing bowl, add the cream cheese, 1/2 cup powdered sugar and lemon pie filling. Using a mixer on medium speed, mix until smooth and combined. Drop the filling, by teaspoonfuls, over the cake batter. Spread the remaining cake batter over the filling.

3. In a mixing bowl, add the brown sugar, pecans, all purpose flour, melted butter, cinnamon and vanilla extract. Stir until combined and sprinkle over the top of the cake batter. Preheat the oven to 350°. Bake for 40 minutes or until a toothpick inserted in the center of the cake comes out clean. Remove the cake from the oven and cool completely before glazing.

4. In a small bowl, add 1/2 cup powdered sugar and lemon juice. Stir until combined and drizzle over the cake.

Lemon Pudding Cake

Ingredients

- 3/4 cup granulated sugar

- 1/8 tsp. salt

- 3 tbs. melted unsalted butter

- 1/4 cup all purpose flour

- 1 tsp. grated lemon zest

- 1/4 cup lemon juice

- 1 1/2 cups whole milk

- 3 beaten egg yolks

- 3 egg whites, beaten to stiff peaks

Directions

1. Preheat the oven to 350°. Spray an 8" square baking pan with non stick cooking spray. In a mixing bowl, add the granulated sugar, salt and butter. Using a mixer on medium speed, beat for 2 minutes. Add the all purpose flour, lemon zest and lemon juice. Mix until well combined.

2. In a small bowl, add the milk and egg yolks. Whisk until combined and add to the mixing bowl. Turn the mixer off and gently fold in the egg whites.

3. Spread the batter into the prepared pan. Place the pan in a 9 x 13 baking pan. Pour hot water around the pan to a depth of 1" on the 8" pan. Bake for 40 minutes or until the top of the cake is lightly browned. Remove the cake from the oven and cool for 15 minutes before serving. Serve the cake warm or chilled.

Blueberry Lemon Cake

Ingredients

- 1/4 cup unsalted butter

- 1/2 cup granulated sugar

- 2 tsp. grated lemon zest

- 2 cups fresh or frozen blueberries

- 9 oz. box yellow cake mix

Directions

1. In a sauce pan over medium heat, add the butter and granulated sugar. Stir constantly and cook until the butter and sugar melt. Remove the pan from the heat and stir in 1 teaspoon lemon zest.

2. Spray an 8" square baking pan with non stick cooking spray. Spread the butter mixture in the bottom of the pan. Sprinkle the blueberries over the top. Prepared the yellow cake mix as directed on the package. Stir 1 teaspoon lemon zest into the cake batter. Spoon the cake batter over the top of the blueberries.

3. Preheat the oven to 350°. Bake for 30 minutes or until a toothpick inserted in the center of the cake comes out clean. Remove the cake from the oven and cool completely before serving.

Peach Upside Down Cake

Ingredients

- 1/4 cup unsalted butter, softened

- 1/2 cup light brown sugar

- 1 1/2 cups canned sliced peaches, drained

- 6 maraschino cherries, halved

- 1/3 cup vegetable shortening

- 1/2 cup granulated sugar

- 1 egg

- 1 1/4 cups cake flour

- 1 1/2 tsp. baking powder

- 1/2 tsp. salt

- 1/2 tsp. grated orange zest

- 1/2 cup orange juice

Directions

1. Preheat the oven to 350°. Spread the butter in the bottom of an 8" round cake pan. Sprinkle the brown sugar over the butter. Spoon the peaches and maraschino cherries over the brown sugar.

2. In a mixing bowl, add the vegetable shortening and granulated sugar. Using a mixer on medium speed, beat for 2 minutes. Add the egg and beat for 2 minutes. Turn the mixer to low. Add the cake flour, baking powder, salt, orange zest and orange juice. Mix only until the batter is combined.

3. Spoon the batter over the peaches. Bake for 45 minutes or until a toothpick inserted in the center of the cake comes out clean. Remove the cake from the oven. Cool the cake for 10 minutes in the pan. Invert the cake onto a serving platter. Cool for 5 minutes before serving.

Fresh Peach Cake

Ingredients

- 2 cups all purpose flour

- 1 tsp. baking soda

- 1 tsp. salt

- 1 tsp. ground cinnamon

- 3 eggs, beaten

- 1 3/4 cups granulated sugar

- 1 cup vegetable oil

- 2 cups sliced fresh peaches

- 1/2 cup chopped pecans

- 2 cups whipped cream

Directions

1. Preheat the oven to 350°. Spray a 9 x 13 baking pan with non stick cooking spray. In a mixing bowl, add 1 1/2 cups all purpose flour, baking soda, salt and cinnamon. Stir until combined.

2. In a separate bowl, add the eggs, granulated sugar and vegetable oil. Using a mixer on medium speed, beat until smooth and combined. Add the dry **Ingredients** and mix until combined. Turn the mixer off. Add 1/2 cup all purpose flour, peaches and pecans to a small bowl. Toss until the peaches and pecans are coated in the flour. Fold the peaches and pecans into the cake batter.

3. Spoon the batter into the prepared pan. Bake for 45 minutes or until a toothpick inserted in the center of the cake comes out clean. Remove the cake from the oven and cool completely before serving. Spoon a dollop of whipped cream over each serving.

Brown Sugar Pudding Cake

Ingredients

- 1/2 cup unsalted butter, softened

- 1 1/2 cups packed light brown sugar

- 1 1/2 cups all purpose flour

- 2 tsp. baking powder

- 1/8 tsp. salt

- 1 tsp. ground nutmeg

- 1 tsp. ground cinnamon

- 1 cup whole milk

- 1/2 cup raisins

- 1 1/2 cups water

Directions

1. In a mixing bowl, add the butter. Using a mixer on medium speed, beat until light and fluffy. Add 1/2 cup brown sugar and mix for 2 minutes. Add the all purpose flour, baking powder, salt, nutmeg, cinnamon and milk. Mix until the batter is smooth and combined. Turn the mixer off and stir in the raisins.

2. Spray a 2 quart souffle dish with non stick cooking spray. Spoon the batter into the dish. In a sauce pan over medium heat, add 1 cup brown sugar and the water. Stir constantly and bring the water to a boil. Remove the pan from the heat. Gently pour the water over the top of the batter. Do not stir.

3. Preheat the oven to 375°. Bake for 40 minutes or until the edges of the cake are golden brown and begin to pull away from the sides. Remove the cake from the oven and cool for 10 minutes before serving.

4. Spoon the cake into dessert dishes. You will have a moist brownie like cake on top and brown sugar sauce on the bottom. The sauce will look thin but will thicken as it cools.

Peanut Butter Cake

Makes a 9 x 13 baking pan

Ingredients

- 1 1/2 cups creamy peanut butter

- 2/3 cup unsalted butter, softened

- 2 cups light brown sugar

- 6 eggs

- 2 cups all purpose flour

- 2 tsp. baking powder

- 1/2 tsp. salt

- 1 1/4 cups plus 1 tbs. whole milk

- 3 tsp. vanilla extract

- 4 cups powdered sugar

- 1/2 cup chopped roasted peanuts

Directions

1. Preheat the oven to 350°. Spray a 9 x 13 baking pan with non stick cooking spray. In a mixing bowl, add 1 cup peanut butter and the butter. Using a mixer on medium speed, beat for 2 minutes. Add the brown sugar and beat for 3 minutes. Add the eggs and beat for 3 minutes.

2. Add the all purpose flour, baking powder, salt, 3/4 cup milk and 2 teaspoons vanilla extract. Beat until the batter is smooth and combined. Spread the batter into the prepared pan. Bake for 45 minutes or until a toothpick inserted in the center of the cake comes out clean. Remove the cake from the oven and cool completely before frosting.

3. In a mixing bowl, add 1/2 cup peanut butter, powdered sugar, 1/2 cup plus 1 tablespoon milk and 1 teaspoon vanilla extract. Using a mixer on medium speed, beat for 5 minutes. The frosting should be smooth and spreadable when ready. Spread the frosting on the cooled cake. Sprinkle the peanuts over the frosting and serve.

Praline Cake

Ingredients

- 1/4 cup vegetable shortening

- 3/4 cup granulated sugar

- 1 egg

- 1 1/2 cups sifted cake flour

- 1 1/2 tsp. baking powder

- 1/4 tsp. salt

- 2/3 cup whole milk

- 1 tsp. vanilla extract

- 1 tbs. plus 1 tsp. all purpose flour

- 1/2 cup light brown sugar

- 1/4 cup melted unsalted butter

- 2 tbs. water

- 3/4 cup chopped pecans

Directions

1. Preheat the oven to 350°. Spray an 8" square baking pan with non stick cooking spray. In a mixing bowl, add the vegetable shortening and granulated sugar. Using a mixer on medium speed, beat for 2 minutes. Add the egg and beat for 2 minutes. Add the cake flour, baking powder, salt, milk and vanilla extract. Beat until the batter is smooth and combined. Spread the batter into the prepared pan.

2. Bake for 25 minutes or until a toothpick inserted in the center of the cake comes out clean. Remove

the cake from the oven and cool the cake for 5 minutes. In a mixing bowl, add the all purpose flour, brown sugar, butter, water and pecans. Stir until well combined and spread over the hot cake. Bake for 5 minutes. Remove the cake from the oven and cool completely before serving.

Southern Vinegar Air Cake

Ingredients

- 4 eggs, separated and at room temperature

- 1 tsp. white vinegar

- 1 cup granulated sugar

- 1 cup cake flour, sifted

- 1 tsp. vanilla extract

Directions

1. It is very important to sift the cake flour in this recipe. I sift the flour twice before using. In a mixing bowl, add the egg yolks. Using a mixer on medium speed, beat for 3 minutes or until the egg yolks are light and fluffy. Add the white vinegar to the yolks and beat until combined.

2. In a separate mixing bowl, add the egg whites. Using a mixer on medium speed, beat until stiff peaks form. Add the egg yolks to the egg whites. Turn the mixer off and gently fold the egg yolks into the egg whites. Add the granulated sugar, cake flour and vanilla extract to the bowl. Gently fold until well combined and the batter is light and fluffy.

3. Preheat the oven to 375°. Spray a 9 x 13 baking pan with non stick cooking spray. Spoon the batter into the pan. Bake for 30 minutes or until a toothpick inserted in the center of the cake comes out clean. Remove the cake from the oven and cool for 10 minutes before serving. This cake is best served warm. I like to spoon fresh strawberries and Cool Whip over the top of the cake. Canned or fresh peaches and blackberries are also good.

Lightning Cake

Ingredients

- 1 cup unsalted butter, softened

- 1 cup granulated sugar

- 4 beaten eggs

- 1 cup all purpose flour

- 1 tsp. baking powder

- 1 tsp. vanilla extract

- Powdered sugar to taste

Directions

1. Preheat the oven to 350°. Grease an 8" square baking pan with 1 tablespoon butter. Add the remaining butter and granulated sugar to a mixing bowl. Using a mixer on medium speed, beat for 3 minutes. Add the eggs and mix until well blended. Add the all purpose flour, baking powder and vanilla extract to the batter. Mix until combined.

2. Spoon the batter into the prepared pan. Bake for 25 minutes or until a toothpick inserted in the center of the cake comes out clean. Remove the cake from the oven and cool completely before serving. Sprinkle powdered sugar to taste over the top of the cake.

Slow Cooker Hot Fudge Cake

Ingredients

- 1 3/4 cups light brown sugar

- 1 cup all purpose flour

- 6 tbs. unsweetened cocoa

- 2 tsp. baking powder

- 1/2 tsp. salt

- 1/2 cup whole milk

- 2 tbs. melted unsalted butter

- 1/2 tsp. vanilla extract

- 1 1/2 cups semisweet chocolate chips

- 1 3/4 cups boiling water

- 3 cups vanilla ice cream

Directions

1. In a mixing bowl, add 1 cup brown sugar, all purpose flour, 3 tablespoons cocoa, baking powder and salt. Stir until combined. Add the milk, butter and vanilla extract. Whisk until smooth and combined. Spray a 4 quart slow cooker with non stick cooking spray. Spoon the batter into the slow cooker.

2. Sprinkle the chocolate chips over the top of the batter. In a mixing bowl, add 3/4 cup brown sugar, 3 tablespoons cocoa and boiling water. Whisk until combined and pour over the batter. Do not stir.

3. Set the temperature to high and cook for 3 1/2 hours or until a toothpick inserted in the center of the cake comes out clean. Spoon the cake into serving bowls and top each serving with 1/2 cup vanilla ice cream.

Depression Cake

Ingredients

- 1 cup vegetable shortening

- 2 cups water

- 2 cups raisins

- 1 tsp. ground cinnamon

- 1 tsp. ground nutmeg

- 1 tsp. allspice

- 1/2 tsp. ground cloves

- 2 cups granulated sugar

- 3 cups all purpose flour

- 1 tsp. baking soda

Directions

1. In a sauce pan over medium heat, add the vegetable shortening, water, raisins, cinnamon, nutmeg, allspice, cloves and granulated sugar. Stir until combined and bring to a boil. When the raisins are boiling, reduce the heat to low. Simmer for 10 minutes. Remove the pan from the heat and let the pan sit at room temperature until the batter is completely cool.

2. When the cake batter is cool, stir in the all purpose flour and baking soda. Mix until the batter is well combined. Preheat the oven to 350°. Spray a 9 x 13 baking pan with non stick cooking spray. Spoon the batter into the pan.

3. Bake for 45 minutes or until a toothpick inserted in the center of the cake comes out clean. Remove the cake from the oven and cool completely before serving.

Old Fashioned Gingerbread

Ingredients

- 1/2 cup unsalted butter, softened

- 1 cup granulated sugar

- 1 cup molasses

- 1 egg

- 2 1/2 cups all purpose flour

- 1 1/2 tsp. baking soda

- 1/2 tsp. salt

- 1 tsp. ground ginger

- 1 tsp. ground cinnamon

- 1 cup hot water

Directions

1. Preheat the oven to 350°. Spray a 9 x 13 baking pan with non stick cooking spray. In a mixing bowl, add the butter and granulated sugar. Using a mixer on medium speed, beat for 3 minutes. Add the molasses and egg. Beat for 3 minutes. Turn the mixer to low speed. Add the all purpose flour, baking soda, salt, ginger, cinnamon and hot water. Mix only until the batter is smooth and combined.

2. Spread the batter into the prepared pan. Bake for 30 minutes or until a toothpick inserted in the center of the gingerbread comes out clean. Remove the pan from the oven. Cool at least 15 minutes before serving.

Short'nin Bread

Ingredients

- 2 cups all purpose flour

- 1/2 tsp. ground cinnamon

- 1/4 tsp. ground nutmeg

- 1 1/2 tsp. baking soda

- 1/2 cup buttermilk

- 1/4 cup plus 2 tbs. unsalted butter

- 1 cup molasses

- 1 beaten egg

Directions

1. In a mixing bowl, add the all purpose flour, cinnamon and nutmeg. Stir until combined. In a small bowl, add the baking soda and buttermilk. Stir until the baking soda melts.

2. In a sauce pan over medium heat, add the butter and molasses. Stir constantly and bring the molasses to a boil Remove the pan from the heat and stir in the dry **Ingredients**. Add the egg and buttermilk to the pan. Stir until combined.

   Spray a 9" cast iron skillet with non stick cooking spray. Spread the batter into the skillet. Preheat the oven to 350°. Bake for 25 minutes or until a toothpick inserted in the center of the bread comes out clean. Remove the skillet from the oven and cool the bread in the skillet for 10 minutes. Invert the bread onto a serving platter. Cut into wedges and serve.

Chocolate Walnut Cake

Ingredients

- 5 oz. unsweetened baking chocolate

- 1/2 cup boiling water

- 1 cup vegetable shortening

- 1 3/4 cups granulated sugar

- 4 eggs

- 3 tsp. vanilla extract

- 2 1/4 cups all purpose flour

- 1 3/4 tsp. salt

- 1 tsp. baking soda

- 1/2 tsp. baking powder

- 1 cup buttermilk

- 1 1/2 cups chopped walnuts

- 6 tbs. unsalted butter, cubed

- 1/3 cup whole milk

- 1/3 cup granulated sugar

- 1 tbs. light corn syrup

Directions

1. In a small bowl, add 3 ounces baking chocolate and the boiling water. Stir until the chocolate melts. Cool for 10 minutes. In a mixing bowl, add the vegetable shortening and 1 3/4 cups granulated sugar. Using a mixer on medium speed, beat for 3 minutes or until the mixture is light and fluffy. Add the eggs and mix for 3 minutes. Add the melted chocolate and 2 teaspoons vanilla extract to the bowl. Mix until smooth and combined.

2. Add the all purpose flour, 1 1/2 teaspoons salt, baking soda, baking powder and buttermilk. Mix only until combined. Turn the mixer off and stir in the walnuts. Preheat the oven to 350°. Spray a 10" bundt pan with non stick cooking spray. Spoon the batter into the pan. Bake for 40 minutes or until a toothpick inserted in the center of the cake comes out clean. Remove the cake from the oven and cool the cake in the pan for 10 minutes. Invert the cake onto a serving plate. Cool the cake completely before frosting.

3. In a sauce pan over low heat, add 2 ounces baking chocolate, butter, whole milk, 1/3 cup granulated sugar, corn syrup, 1/4 teaspoon salt and 1 teaspoon vanilla extract. Stir constantly and cook until the chocolate melts and the frosting is smooth. Remove the pan from the heat and add the frosting to a mixing bowl. Using a mixer on medium speed, beat for 15 minutes. Refrigerate the frosting until the frosting firms up slightly and is spreadable. Spread the frosting on the top and sides of the cake.

Black Walnut Cake

Ingredients

- 1 1/4 cups unsalted butter, softened

- 1/2 cup vegetable shortening

- 2 cups light brown sugar

- 1 cup granulated sugar

- 5 eggs

- 3 cups all purpose flour

- 1/2 tsp. baking powder

- 1/4 tsp. salt

- 1 cup plus 3 tbs. whole milk

- 1 tsp. vanilla extract

- 1 cup finely chopped black walnuts

- 3 oz. cream cheese, softened

- 2 cups powdered sugar

Directions

1. Preheat the oven to 325°. Spray a 10" bundt pan with non stick cooking spray. In a mixing bowl, add 1 cup butter and vegetable shortening. Using a mixer on medium speed, beat until smooth and combined. Add the brown sugar and granulated sugar to the bowl. Beat for 3 minutes or until combined and fluffy.

2. Add the eggs, one at a time, to the bowl. Make sure each egg is incorporated into the batter before adding the next egg. Add the all purpose flour, baking powder, salt, 1 cup milk and vanilla extract to the batter. Mix only until combined. Turn the mixer off and stir in the black walnuts. Spoon the batter into the prepared pan.

3. Bake for 1 1/2 hours or until a toothpick inserted in the center of the cake comes out clean. Remove the cake from the oven and cool the cake in the pan for 15 minutes. Remove the cake from the pan and cool completely before frosting.

4. In a mixing bowl, add 1/4 cup butter, cream cheese, powdered sugar and 2 tablespoons milk. Using a mixer on medium speed, beat until smooth and fluffy. Add the remaining milk if needed to make a fluffy frosting. Spread the frosting over the cooled cake and serve. Store the cake in the refrigerator.

Orange Walnut Cake

Ingredients

- 1 cup unsalted butter, softened

- 2 cups granulated sugar

- 5 eggs, separated and at room temperature

- 3 cups all purpose flour

- 1 tbs. baking powder

- 2 tsp. grated orange zest

- 1/2 tsp. ground nutmeg

- 1 cup plus 2 tbs. whole milk

- 1 cup chopped walnuts

- 8 oz. pkg. cream cheese, softened

- 4 cups powdered sugar

- 1 tsp. vanilla extract

Directions

1. Preheat the oven to 350°. Spray a 9 x 13 baking pan with non stick cooking spray. In a mixing bowl, add the butter and granulated sugar. Using a mixer on medium speed, beat for 4 minutes. Add the egg yolks and beat for 3 minutes. Add the all purpose flour, baking powder, orange zest, nutmeg and 1 cup milk. Mix until combined. Turn the mixer off and fold in the walnuts.

2. In a mixing bowl, add the egg whites. Using a mixer on medium speed, beat until stiff peaks form. Gently fold the egg whites into the cake batter. Spread the batter into the prepared pan. Bake for 45 minutes or until a toothpick inserted in the center of the cake comes out clean. Remove the cake from the oven and cool the cake in the pan for 15 minutes. Remove the cake from the pan and cool completely before frosting.

3. In a mixing bowl, add the cream cheese. Using a mixer on medium speed, beat for 1 minute. Add 2 tablespoons milk, powdered sugar and vanilla extract. Beat for 5 minutes or until the frosting is thick and spreadable. Spread the frosting on the cooled cake.

Pecan Cake

Ingredients

- 12 tbs. unsalted butter, softened

- 3 cups granulated sugar

- 6 eggs, separated and at room temperature

- 2 oz. lemon extract

- 3 cups all purpose flour

- 4 cups whole pecans

- 1 lb. raisins

Directions

1. Preheat the oven to 225°. Spray a 10" tube pan with non stick cooking spray. In a mixing bowl, add the butter and granulated sugar. Using a mixer on medium speed, beat for 3 minutes. The mixture should be light and fluffy when ready.

2. Add the egg yolks, one at a time, to the bowl. Make sure the egg yolks are well combined before adding the next egg yolk. Add the lemon extract and mix until combined. Add the all purpose flour, pecans and raisins. Mix until combined. The batter will be thick.

3. In a separate mixing bowl, add the egg whites. Using a mixer on medium speed, beat until stiff peaks form. Fold the egg whites into the batter. Spoon the batter into the prepared pan. Bake for 3 hours or until a toothpick inserted in the center of the cake comes out clean. Remove the cake from the oven and cool the cake in the pan for 10 minutes. Remove the cake from the pan and invert the cake onto a serving platter. Cool the cake for 12 hours before serving.

Lemon Gold Cake

Ingredients

- 2 1/2 cups all purpose flour

- 1 1/2 cups granulated sugar

- 1 tbs. baking powder

- 1 1/8 tsp. salt

- 1/2 cup vegetable oil

- 6 eggs, separated and at room temperature

- 3/4 cup water

- 3 tsp. grated lemon zest

- 3 tbs. plus 2 tsp. lemon juice

- 1/2 tsp. cream of tartar

- 1/2 cup unsalted butter, softened

- 4 cups powdered sugar

Directions

1. In a mixing bowl, add the all purpose flour, granulated sugar, baking powder and salt. Stir until combined. Add the vegetable oil, egg yolks, water, 1 teaspoon lemon zest and 2 teaspoons lemon juice. Using a mixer on high speed, beat for 5 minutes. The batter should be smooth and glossy.

2. In a separate mixing bowl, add the egg whites and cream of tartar. Using a mixer on medium speed, beat until stiff peaks form. Fold the egg whites into the cake batter. The key to the cake is the folding of the egg whites. Gently fold so you do not deflate the egg whites.

3. Spoon the batter into an ungreased 10" tube pan. Bake for 50 minutes or until the top of the cake springs back when touched. Remove the cake from the oven. Cool the cake completely in the pan.

4. In a mixing bowl, add the butter and 2 cups powdered sugar. Using a mixer on medium speed, beat until smooth. Add 2 cups powdered sugar, 2 teaspoons lemon zest and 3 tablespoons lemon juice. Beat for 4 minutes or until the frosting is smooth and spreadable. Remove the cake from the pan and

place on a serving platter. Spread the frosting over the top and sides of the cake.

Lemon Pecan Cake

Ingredients

- 2 cups unsalted butter, softened

- 2 1/4 cups light brown sugar

- 6 eggs, separated and at room temperature

- 4 cups all purpose flour

- 1 1/4 tsp. baking powder

- 1/4 tsp. salt

- 1/2 cup whole milk

- 2 tbs. plus 2 tsp. lemon extract

- 4 cups chopped pecans

Directions

1. Preheat the oven to 325°. Spray a 10" tube pan with non stick cooking spray. In a mixing bowl, add the butter and brown sugar. Using a mixer on medium speed, beat for 3 minutes. The mixture should be light and fluffy when ready.

2. Add the egg yolks, one at a time, to the bowl. Make sure the egg yolks are well combined before adding the next egg yolk. Add the all purpose flour, baking powder, salt and milk. Mix until combined. The batter will be thick. Turn the mixer off and fold in the lemon extract and pecans.

3. In a separate mixing bowl, add the egg whites. Using a mixer on medium speed, beat until stiff peaks form. Fold the egg whites into the batter. Spoon the batter into the prepared pan. Bake for 1 1/4 hours or until a toothpick inserted in the center of the cake comes out clean. Remove the cake from the oven and cool for 10 minutes in the pan. Invert the cake onto a serving platter. Cool the cake for 12 hours before serving.

Angel Food Cake

Ingredients

- 12 egg whites, at room temperature

- 1 1/2 tsp. cream of tartar

- 1/4 tsp. salt

- 1 1/2 cups granulated sugar

- 1 cup sifted cake flour

- 1 1/2 tsp. vanilla extract

Directions

1. Add the egg whites to a mixing bowl. Using a mixer on medium speed, beat until the egg whites are foamy. Add the cream of tartar and salt to the bowl. Beat until soft peaks form. Add the granulated sugar, 2 tablespoons at a time, to the egg whites. Beat until stiff peaks form and the sugar dissolves. Turn the mixer off.

2. Sprinkle the cake flour over the egg whites. Gently fold the flour into the egg whites. Add the vanilla extract and fold until well blended. Preheat the oven to 375°. Spoon the batter into an ungreased 10" tube pan. Run a knife through the cake batter to remove air bubbles.

3. Bake for 30 minutes or until the top of the cake springs back lightly when touched. Remove the cake from the oven. Invert the cake onto a wire cooling rack. Let the cake cool for 40 minutes. Run a knife around the edges and tube part of the pan to loosen the cake. Invert the cake onto a serving platter. Cool completely before serving.

Chocolate Angel Food Cake

Ingredients

- 12 egg whites, at room temperature

- 1 1/2 tsp. cream of tartar

- 1/4 tsp. salt

- 1 1/2 cups granulated sugar

- 1 cup sifted cake flour

- 1/4 cup unsweetened baking cocoa

- 1 1/2 tsp. vanilla extract

Directions

1. Add the egg whites to a mixing bowl. Using a mixer on medium speed, beat until the egg whites are foamy. Add the cream of tartar and salt to the bowl. Beat until soft peaks form. Add the granulated sugar, 2 tablespoons at a time, to the egg whites. Beat until stiff peaks form and the sugar dissolves. Turn the mixer off.

2. Sprinkle the cake flour and cocoa over the egg whites. Gently fold the flour and cocoa into the egg whites. Add the vanilla extract and fold until well blended. Preheat the oven to 375°. Spoon the batter into an ungreased 10" tube pan. Run a knife through the cake batter to remove air bubbles.

3. Bake for 30 minutes or until the top of the cake springs back lightly when touched. Remove the cake from the oven. Invert the cake onto a wire cooling rack. Let the cake cool for 40 minutes. Run a knife around the edges and tube part of the pan to loosen the cake. Invert the cake onto a serving platter. Cool completely before serving.

Brown Sugar Angel Food Cake

Ingredients

1 1/2 cups egg whites, about 12 egg whites

- 1 1/2 tsp. cream of tartar

- 1 tsp. salt

- 2 tsp. vanilla extract

- 2 cups light brown sugar

- 1 1/4 cups sifted cake flour

Directions

1. Add the egg whites to a mixing bowl. Using a mixer on medium speed, beat until the egg whites are foamy. Add the cream of tartar, salt and vanilla extract to the bowl. Beat until soft peaks form. Add 1 cup brown sugar, 2 tablespoons at a time, to the egg whites. Beat until stiff peaks form and the sugar dissolves. Turn the mixer off.

2. In a small bowl, add the cake flour and 1 cup brown sugar. Stir until combined. Sprinkle the cake flour mixture over the egg whites. Gently fold the flour mixture into the egg whites. Preheat the oven to 350°. Spoon the batter into an ungreased 10" tube pan. Run a knife through the cake batter to remove air bubbles.

3. Bake for 45 minutes or until the top of the cake springs back lightly when touched. Remove the cake from the oven. Invert the cake onto a wire cooling rack. Let the cake cool for 40 minutes. Run a knife around the edges and tube part of the pan to loosen the cake. Invert the cake onto a serving platter. Cool completely before serving.

Chocolate Chip Coconut Angel Food Cake

Ingredients

- 1 1/2 cups egg whites, at room temperature

- 1 1/2 cups plus 2 tbs. powdered sugar

- 1 cup cake flour

- 1 1/2 tsp. cream of tartar

- 1 tsp. almond extract

- 1 tsp. vanilla extract

- 1/4 tsp. salt

- 1 cup granulated sugar

- 1 cup miniature semisweet chocolate chips

- 1/2 cup sweetened flaked coconut

- 1 cup heavy whipping cream

- 1/2 cup toasted flaked coconut

Directions

1. 1 1/2 cups egg whites equals about 12 egg whites. Add the egg whites to a mixing bowl. In a small bowl, add 1 1/2 cups powdered sugar and cake flour. Stir until combined.

2. Add the cream of tartar, almond extract, vanilla extract and salt to the egg whites. Using a mixer on medium speed, beat until soft peaks form. Add the granulated sugar, 2 tablespoons at a time, to the egg whites. Beat until the egg whites are glossy and the sugar dissolves. Add the powdered sugar mixture, 1/2 cup at a time, until well combined. Turn the mixer off and gently fold in the chocolate chips and 1/2 cup sweetened flaked coconut.

3. Spoon the batter into an ungreased 10" tube pan. Preheat the oven to 325°. Bake for 50 minutes or until the top springs back lightly when touched and the top begins to crack. Remove the pan from the oven and immediately invert the pan onto a serving plate. Let the cake sit for 10 minutes. Remove the cake from the pan and cool completely before serving.

4. In a mixing bowl, add the heavy whipping cream. Using a mixer on medium speed, beat until stiff peaks form. Gently fold in 1/2 cup toasted coconut. Spoon the whipped cream over slices of the cake.

Vanilla Sponge Cake

Ingredients

1 cup sifted cake flour

- 1 1/4 cups granulated sugar

- 4 egg yolks, at room temperature

- 1 tsp. vanilla extract

- 10 egg whites, at room temperature

- 1 tsp. cream of tartar

- 1/2 tsp. salt

Directions

1. Sift together the cake flour and 1/2 cup granulated sugar. Sift the mixture 3 times. Do not skip this step as this will be crucial to the texture of the cake. Add the egg yolks to a mixing bowl. Using a mixer on medium high speed, beat for 4 minutes. Add the vanilla extract and beat for 4 minutes. The yolks will be thick at this point.

2. In a separate mixing bowl, add the egg whites. Using a mixer on high speed, beat until the egg

whites are foamy. Add the cream of tartar and salt to the bowl. Beat until soft peaks form. Add 3/4 cup granulated sugar, 2 tablespoons at a time, mixing until stiff peaks form. Turn the mixer off.

3. Add the flour mixture, 1/4 at a time to the bowl. Fold the flour into the egg whites before adding additional flour. Gently fold the egg yolks into the egg whites. Spoon the batter into an ungreased 10" tube pan.

4. Preheat the oven to 350°. Bake for 45 minutes or until the top of the cakes springs back lightly when touched. Remove the cake from the oven and cool the cake in the pan for 40 minutes. Using a small metal spatula, loosen the cake from the pan. Invert the cake onto a serving platter. Cool completely before serving.

Chiffon Cake

Ingredients

- 1 cup all purpose flour

- 1 1/2 tsp. baking powder

- 1/4 tsp. salt

- 1 cup granulated sugar

- 1/4 cup vegetable oil

- 4 eggs, separated and at room temperature

- 1/4 cup water

- 1 tsp. vanilla extract

- 1/2 tsp. cream of tartar

Directions

1. Preheat the oven to 325°. In a mixing bowl, add the all purpose flour, baking powder, salt and 1/2 cup granulated sugar. Stir until combined. Add the vegetable oil, egg yolks, water and vanilla extract to the bowl. Using a mixer on high speed, beat for 5 minutes. The batter should be smooth and glossy.

2. In a separate mixing bowl, add the egg whites and cream of tartar. Using a mixer on medium speed, beat until soft peaks form. Add 1/2 cup granulated sugar, 2 tablespoons at a time, to the egg whites. Beat until stiff peaks form. Fold the egg whites into the cake batter. The key to the cake is the folding of the egg whites. Gently fold so you do not deflate the egg whites.

3. Spoon the batter into an ungreased 10" tube pan. Bake for 1 hour or until the top of the cake springs back when touched. Remove the cake from the oven. Invert the pan onto a serving plate. Do not remove the pan. Let the cake sit for 40 minutes. Run a small metal spatula around the cake to loosen the cake from the pan. Remove the cake from the pan. Cool completely before serving.

Lemon Chiffon Cake

Ingredients

- 7 eggs, separated at room temperature
- 1/2 tsp. cream of tartar
- 2 cups all purpose flour
- 1 1/2 cups granulated sugar
- 3 tsp. baking powder
- 1 tsp. salt
- 3/4 cup water
- 1/2 cup vegetable oil
- 4 tsp. grated lemon zest
- 2 tsp. vanilla extract
- Lemon Glaze below

Directions

1. Preheat the oven to 325°. Place 7 egg whites and the cream of tartar in a large mixing bowl. Using a mixer on medium speed, beat until stiff peaks form. Set aside.

2. In a mixing bowl, stir together the all purpose flour, granulated sugar, baking powder and salt. In a separate bowl, add the egg yolks, water, oil, lemon zest and vanilla extract. Using a mixer on medium speed, beat for 3 minutes. Pour the egg mixture into the flour and mix until the cake batter is well combined.

3. Carefully fold the egg whites into the batter. Be careful to fold the egg whites slowly as to not break down the egg whites. The beaten egg whites are what make the cake light.

4. Gently spoon the batter into an ungreased 10" tube pan. Swirl a knife through the batter to remove air pockets. Bake on the lowest oven rack about 50-55 minutes or until the cake springs back when touched. Do not over bake this cake as it will be dense and not as moist.

5. Remove the cake from the oven. Run a knife around the edges and the center of the pan if needed to loosen the cake. Immediately, invert the pan onto a serving plate and cool at least 2 hours. Keep the cake pan on the cake until it falls out of the pan. Ice with lemon glaze below when cool.

6. Lemon Glaze: In a small bowl, add 6 tbs. melted unsalted butter, 2 cups powdered sugar, 1 teaspoon vanilla extract and 3 tablespoons lemon juice. Whisk all the **Ingredients** together and spoon over the cooled cake.

Chocolate Chiffon Cake

Ingredients

- 1 1/2 cups sifted cake flour
- 2 1/4 cups granulated sugar
- 2/3 cup unsweetened baking cocoa
- 1 tsp. baking soda
- 1/2 tsp. salt
- 1/4 cup plus 3 tbs. vegetable oil
- 8 eggs, separated
- 3/4 cup water
- 1 tsp. vanilla extract
- 1 cup whipping cream
- 1/4 cup powdered sugar

Directions

1. In a mixing bowl, add the cake flour, 1 3/4 cups granulated sugar, cocoa, baking soda and salt. Stir until combined. Add the vegetable oil, egg yolks, water and vanilla extract to the bowl. Using a mixer on high speed, beat for 5 minutes. The batter should be smooth and glossy.

2. In a separate mixing bowl, add the egg whites. Using a mixer on medium speed, beat until soft peaks form. Add 1/2 cup granulated sugar, 2 tablespoons at a time, to the egg whites. Beat until stiff peaks form. Fold the egg whites into the cake batter. The key to the cake is the folding of the egg whites. Gently fold so you do not deflate the egg whites.

3. Spoon the batter into an ungreased 10" tube pan. Bake for 1 hour or until the top of the cake springs back when touched. Remove the cake from the oven. Cool the cake completely before removing from the pan.

4. In a mixing bowl, add the whipping cream and powdered sugar. Using a mixer on medium speed, beat until soft peaks form. Invert the cake onto a serving platter. Spread the whipped cream over the top and sides of the cake. Store the cake in the refrigerator.

Coffee Chiffon Cake

Ingredients

- 1 cup all purpose flour
- 1 1/2 tsp. baking powder
- 1/4 tsp. salt

- 1 cup granulated sugar

- 1 teaspoon instant coffee granules

- 1/4 cup water

- 1/4 cup vegetable oil

- 4 eggs, separated and at room temperature

- 1 tsp. vanilla extract

- 1/2 tsp. cream of tartar

- 1/4 cup unsalted butter, softened

- 8 oz. cream cheese, softened

- 3 oz. unsweetened baking chocolate, melted and cooled

- 1/4 cup Kahlua

- 4 cups powdered sugar

Directions

1. Preheat the oven to 325°. In a mixing bowl, add the all purpose flour, baking powder, salt and 1/2 cup granulated sugar. Stir until combined. In a small bowl, add the coffee granules and water. Stir until the coffee dissolves. Add the vegetable oil, egg yolks, coffee and vanilla extract to the dry **Ingredients**. Using a mixer on high speed, beat for 5 minutes. The batter should be smooth and glossy.

2. In a separate mixing bowl, add the egg whites and cream of tartar. Using a mixer on medium speed, beat until soft peaks form. Add 1/2 cup granulated sugar, 2 tablespoons at a time, to the egg whites. Beat until stiff peaks form. Fold the egg whites into the cake batter. The key to the cake is the folding of the egg whites. Gently fold so you do not deflate the egg whites.

3. Spoon the batter into an ungreased 10" tube pan. Bake for 1 hour or until the top of the cake springs back when touched. Remove the cake from the oven. Invert the pan onto a serving plate. Do not remove the pan. Let the cake sit for 40 minutes. Run a small metal spatula around the cake to loosen the cake from the pan. Remove the cake from the pan. Cool completely before frosting.

4. In a mixing bowl, add the butter and cream cheese. Using a mixer on medium speed, beat until light and fluffy. Add the melted chocolate, 1/4 cup Kahlua and 1 cup powdered sugar to the bowl. Mix until smooth and combined. Add enough of the remaining powdered sugar to make a spreadable frosting. Frost the cooled cake.

Praline Chiffon Cake

Ingredients

- 2 cups all purpose flour

- 3/4 cup granulated sugar

- 3/4 cup light brown sugar

- 1 tbs. baking powder

- 1/2 tsp. salt

- 1/2 cup vegetable oil

- 7 eggs, separated and at room temperature

- 3/4 cup cold water

- 2 tsp. maple flavoring

- 1 tsp. cream of tartar

Directions

1. In a mixing bowl, add the all purpose flour, granulated sugar, brown sugar, baking powder and salt. Stir until combined. Add the vegetable oil, egg yolks, water and maple flavoring to the bowl. Using a mixer on high speed, beat for 5 minutes. The batter should be smooth and glossy.

2. In a separate mixing bowl, add the egg whites and cream of tartar. Using a mixer on medium speed, beat until stiff peaks form. Fold the egg whites into the cake batter. The key to the cake is the folding of the egg whites. Gently fold so you do not deflate the egg whites.

3. Spoon the batter into an ungreased 10" tube pan. Bake for 1 hour or until the top of the cake springs back when touched. Remove the cake from the oven and invert the pan onto a serving platter. Leave the pan on the cake for 40 minutes. Remove the pan and cool the cake completely before serving.

Marble Chiffon Cake

Ingredients

- 2 1/4 cups sifted cake flour

- 1 1/2 cups plus 2 tbs. granulated sugar

- 3 tsp. baking powder

- 1 tsp. salt

- 1/2 cup vegetable oil

- 7 egg yolks, at room temperature

- 3/4 cup cold water

- 1 tsp. vanilla extract

- 7 egg whites, at room temperature

- 1/2 tsp. cream of tartar

- 1/4 cup boiling water

- 2 oz. unsweetened baking chocolate, melted

Directions

1. In a large mixing bowl, add the cake flour, 1 1/2 cups granulated sugar, baking powder and salt. Stir until combined. Add the vegetable oil, egg yolks, cold water and vanilla extract to the bowl. Using a mixer on medium speed, beat for 5 minutes. The batter should be glossy and smooth.

2. In a separate mixing bowl, add the egg whites and cream of tartar. Using a mixer on medium speed, beat until stiff peaks form. Fold the egg whites into the cake batter. The key to the cake is the folding of the egg whites. Gently fold so you do not deflate the egg whites. Remove 1/3 of the cake batter and place in a mixing bowl.

3. Spoon half the remaining batter into an ungreased 10" tube pan. In a small bowl, add the boiling water, 2 tablespoons granulated sugar and melted chocolate. Stir until combined and add to the reserved 1/3 cake batter. Spread half the chocolate batter over the white layer. Repeat the layering process one more time. Using a knife, gently swirl the batters to create a marbled effect.

4. Preheat the oven to 325°. Bake for 50 minutes or until a toothpick inserted in the center of the cake comes out clean. Remove the cake from the oven. Invert the pan onto a serving plate. Do not remove the pan. Let the cake sit for 40 minutes. Run a small metal spatula around the cake to loosen the cake from the pan. Remove the cake from the pan. Cool completely before serving. This is very good covered in chocolate frosting.

Tropical Chiffon Cake

Ingredients

- 2 1/4 cups sifted cake flour

- 1 1/2 cups granulated sugar

- 3 tsp. baking powder

- 1 tsp. salt

- 1 cup vegetable oil

- 3/4 cup egg yolks, or about 8 egg yolks

- 1 tsp. grated orange zest

- 3/4 cup orange juice

- 1 cup egg whites, or about 8 egg whites

- 1/2 tsp. cream of tartar

- 1 1/3 cups sweetened flaked coconut

Directions

1. In a large mixing bowl, add the cake flour, granulated sugar, baking powder and salt. Stir until combined. Add the vegetable oil, egg yolks, orange zest and orange juice to the bowl. Using a mixer on medium speed, beat for 5 minutes. The batter should be glossy and smooth.

2. In a separate mixing bowl, add the egg whites and cream of tartar. Using a mixer on medium speed, beat until stiff peaks form. Turn the mixer off. Fold the egg whites into the cake batter. The key to the cake is the folding of the egg whites. Gently fold so you do not deflate the egg whites. Fold the coconut into the cake batter.

3. Spoon the batter into an ungreased 10" tube pan. Preheat the oven to 325°. Bake for 50 minutes or until a toothpick inserted in the center of the cake comes out clean. Remove the cake from the oven. Invert the pan onto a serving plate. Do not remove the pan. Let the cake sit for 40 minutes. Run a small metal spatula around the cake to loosen the cake from the pan. Remove the cake from the pan. Cool completely before serving. Very good with an orange, lemon or citrus glaze.

Orange Sunshine Cake

Ingredients

- 3/4 cup egg yolks, about 8 egg yolks

- 1 1/2 cups granulated sugar

- 1 tsp. grated orange zest

- 1/2 cup orange juice

- 1 cup sifted cake flour

- 1 cup egg whites, about 8 egg whites

- 1 tsp. cream of tartar

- 1/2 tsp. salt

Directions

1. In a mixing bowl, add the egg yolks. Using a mixer on medium speed, beat for 4 minutes. The egg yolks should be thick and lemon colored when ready. With the mixer running, slowly add 3/4 cup granulated sugar. Beat for 3 minutes. Add the orange zest, orange juice and cake flour to the bowl. Mix until combined.

2. In a separate mixing bowl, add the egg whites, cream of tartar and salt. Using a mixer on medium speed, beat until soft peaks form. With the mixer running, slowly add 3/4 cup granulated sugar. Mix until stiff peaks form.

3. Fold the egg whites into the cake batter. The key to the cake is the folding of the egg whites. Gently fold so you do not deflate the egg whites. Spoon the batter into an ungreased 10" tube pan.

4. Preheat the oven to 325°. Bake for 1 hour or until a toothpick inserted in the center of the cake comes out clean. Remove the cake from the oven. Invert the pan onto a serving plate. Do not remove the pan. Let the cake sit for 40 minutes. Run a small metal spatula around the cake to loosen the cake from the pan. Remove the cake from the pan. Cool completely before serving. Very good with an

orange, lemon or citrus glaze.

Cranberry Pear Bundt Cake

Ingredients

- 1 cup light brown sugar

- 3/4 cup chopped pecans

- 1/3 cup dried cranberries

- 1 1/4 tsp. apple pie spice

- 1/2 cup unsalted butter, softened

- 1 cup granulated sugar

- 3 eggs

- 1 1/4 tsp. vanilla extract

- 2 cups all purpose flour

- 2 tsp. baking powder

- 1 tsp. baking soda

- 1/2 tsp. salt

- 1 cup sour cream

- 2 cups peeled pears, chopped

- 1 cup powdered sugar

- 5 tsp. whole milk

- 4 1/2 tsp. melted unsalted butter

Directions

1. In a small bowl, add the brown sugar, pecans, cranberries and 1 teaspoon apple pie spice. Stir until combined. In a large mixing bowl, add 1/2 cup softened butter and granulated sugar. Using a mixer on medium speed, beat for 3 minutes. Add the eggs and 1 teaspoon vanilla extract to the bowl. Beat for 3 minutes. Add the all purpose flour, baking powder, baking soda, salt and sour cream to the batter. Mix only until combined. Turn the mixer off and fold in the pears.

2. Preheat the oven to 350°. Spray a 10" bundt pan with non stick cooking spray. Spoon half the cake batter into the pan. Sprinkle the pecan mixture over the cake batter. Spoon the remaining cake batter into the pan. Bake for 45 minutes or until a toothpick inserted in the center of the cake comes out clean. Remove the cake from the oven and cool the cake for 10 minutes in the pan.

3. Invert the pan onto a serving platter. Cool the cake completely before glazing. In a small bowl, add

the powdered sugar, milk, melted butter, 1/4 teaspoon apple pie spice and 1/4 teaspoon vanilla extract. Whisk until combined and spoon over the cooled cake.

Sweet Potato Cake

Ingredients

- 2/3 cup unsalted butter, softened
- 2 cups granulated sugar
- 4 eggs, separated and at room temperature
- 1 cup mashed cooked sweet potato
- 2 cups all purpose flour
- 1 tsp. baking soda
- 1/2 tsp. salt
- 2 tbs. unsweetened baking cocoa
- 1 tsp. ground allspice
- 1 tsp. ground cinnamon
- 1 tsp. ground cloves
- 1 tsp. ground nutmeg
- 1 cup buttermilk
- 1 tsp. vanilla extract
- 1 1/2 cups seedless raisins
- 2 cups chopped pecans
- 1 cup powdered sugar

Directions

1. Preheat the oven to 325°. Spray a 10" tube pan with non stick cooking spray. In a mixing bowl, add the butter and granulated sugar. Using a mixer on medium speed, beat for 3 minutes. Add the egg yolks and sweet potato. Mix until smooth and combined.

2. Add the all purpose flour, baking soda, salt, cocoa, allspice, cinnamon, cloves, nutmeg, buttermilk and vanilla extract. Mix until the batter is well combined. Turn the mixer off and stir in the raisins and pecans. Spoon the batter into the pan. Add the egg whites to a mixing bowl. Using a mixer on medium speed, beat until stiff peaks form. Fold the egg whites into the cake batter.

3. Spoon the batter into the prepared pan. Bake for 1 1/4 hours or until a toothpick inserted in the center of the cake comes out clean. Remove the cake from the oven. Cool the cake in the pan for 10

minutes. Invert the cake onto a serving platter. Cool the cake completely. Sift the powdered sugar over the top of the cake and serve.

Fig Preserve Cake

Ingredients

- 2 1/2 cups granulated sugar

- 2 cups all purpose flour

- 2 1/2 tsp. baking soda

- 1/2 tsp. salt

- 1 tsp. ground nutmeg

- 1 tsp. ground cinnamon

- 1 1/2 tsp. ground allspice

- 1/4 tsp. ground cloves

- 1 cup vegetable oil

- 3 eggs

- 1 cup buttermilk

- 1 tbs. plus 1 tsp. vanilla extract

- 1 cup fig preserves

- 1 cup chopped pecans

- 1/2 cup unsalted butter, softened

- 1/2 cup whole milk

- 1 tbs. light corn syrup

Directions

1. Preheat the oven to 350°. Spray a 10" bundt pan with non stick cooking spray. In a mixing bowl, add 1 1/2 cups granulated sugar, all purpose flour, 1 teaspoon baking soda, salt, nutmeg, cinnamon, allspice and cloves. Stir until combined.

2. Add the vegetable oil, eggs, buttermilk and 1 tablespoon vanilla extract to the bowl. Using a mixer on medium speed, beat until the cake batter is smooth and combined. Turn the mixer off and stir in the fig preserves and pecans. Spoon the batter into the pan.

3. Bake for 1 hour or until a toothpick inserted in the center of the cake comes out clean. Remove the cake from the oven and cool the cake in the pan for 10 minutes. Invert the cake onto a serving platter. Cool the cake for 30 minutes before glazing.

4. To make the glaze, add the butter, 1 cup granulated sugar, 1 1/2 teaspoons baking soda, milk, corn syrup and 1 teaspoon vanilla extract to a dutch oven. Stir constantly and bring the glaze to a boil. Continue stirring and cook until the glaze turns golden brown. Remove the pan from the heat and cool until the glaze is lukewarm. Spoon the glaze over the cake while the cake is still warm. Let the cake sit for 8 hours before serving.

Fresh Apple Cake

Ingredients

- 2 cups granulated sugar
- 1 1/2 cups vegetable oil
- 3 eggs
- 2 tsp. vanilla extract
- 3 cups all purpose flour
- 1 tsp. baking soda
- 1 tsp. salt
- 1 tsp. ground cinnamon
- 3 cups peeled, diced apples
- 1 cup chopped pecans
- 1 cup light brown sugar
- 1/2 cup unsalted butter
- 1/4 cup evaporated milk

Directions

1. Preheat the oven to 325°. Spray a 10" tube pan with non stick cooking spray. In a mixing bowl, add the granulated sugar, vegetable oil, eggs and vanilla extract. Using a mixer on medium speed, beat for 3 minutes.

2. Add 2 1/2 cups all purpose flour, baking soda, salt and cinnamon to the bowl. Mix until combined. In a small bowl, add 1/2 cup all purpose flour, apples and pecans. Toss until the apples and pecans are coated in the all purpose flour. Add the apples and pecans to the bowl. Mix only until combined.

3. Spoon the batter into the prepared pan. Bake for 1 1/4 hours or until a toothpick inserted in the center of the cake comes out clean. Remove the cake from the oven and cool the cake in the pan for 15 minutes. Remove the cake from the pan and cool completely before frosting.

4. In a sauce pan over medium heat, add the brown sugar, butter and evaporated milk. Stir constantly and cook until the temperature reaches 240° on a candy thermometer. Remove the pan from the heat. With a heavy spoon, beat for 5 minutes or until the frosting is thick enough to spread. Spread the frosting over the top of the cake.

Applesauce Cake

Ingredients

- 1 cup unsalted butter
- 2 cups light brown sugar
- 1 egg
- 3 cups all purpose flour
- 2 tsp. baking soda
- 1/4 tsp. salt
- 1 tsp. ground cinnamon
- 1 tsp. ground cloves
- 2 cups applesauce
- 2 cups raisins
- 1 cup chopped walnuts

Directions

1. Preheat the oven to 350°. In a mixing bowl, add the butter and brown sugar. Using a mixer on medium speed, beat for 4 minutes. Add the egg and beat for 2 minutes.

2. Add 2 1/2 cups all purpose flour, baking soda, salt, cinnamon, cloves and applesauce. Mix until the batter is smooth and combined. In a small bowl, add 1/2 cup all purpose flour, raisins and walnuts. Toss until the raisins and walnuts are coated in the flour. Add the mixture to the batter. Stir until combined.

3. Spray a 10" tube pan with non stick cooking spray. Spoon the batter into the pan. Bake for 1 1/4 hours or until a toothpick inserted in the center of the cake comes out clean. Remove the cake from the oven. Cool the cake in the pan for 15 minutes. Remove the cake from the pan and let the cake rest at least 8 hours before serving.

Vanilla Bundt Cake

Ingredients

- 1 cup vegetable shortening
- 2 cups granulated sugar
- 4 eggs
- 2 tbs. plus 1/2 tsp. vanilla extract
- 3 cups all purpose flour

- 1 tsp. baking powder

- 1/2 tsp. baking soda

- 1 cup buttermilk

- 1 cup powdered sugar

- 2 tbs. whole milk

Directions

1. Preheat the oven to 350°. Spray a 10" bundt pan with non stick cooking spray. In a mixing bowl, add the vegetable shortening and granulated sugar. Using a mixer on medium speed, beat for 5 minutes. Add the eggs and 2 tablespoons vanilla extract. Beat for 4 minutes. Add the all purpose flour, baking powder, baking soda and buttermilk to the bowl. Mix only until the batter is combined.

2. Spoon the batter into the bundt pan. Bake for 1 hour or until a toothpick inserted in the center of the cake comes out clean. Remove the cake from the oven and cool the cake in the pan for 10 minutes. Invert the cake onto a serving platter and cool completely.

3. In a mixing bowl, add the powdered sugar, 1/2 teaspoon vanilla extract and 1 tablespoon milk. Whisk until combined and a smooth glaze forms. Add the remaining 1 tablespoon milk if needed to make a smooth glaze. Drizzle the glaze over the cooled cake.

Old Fashioned Pound Cake

Ingredients

- 2 cups unsalted butter

- 3 cups granulated sugar

- 6 eggs

- 2 tsp. vanilla extract

- 1 tsp. lemon juice

- 4 cups all purpose flour

- 3/4 cup whole milk

Directions

1. All **Ingredients** must be at room temperature. A great pound cake requires thorough mixing. Preheat the oven to 350°. In a large mixing bowl, add the butter. Using a mixer on medium speed, beat the butter until light and fluffy or about 3 minutes. Do not skip this step. Add the granulated sugar and beat for 2 minutes. Add the eggs, vanilla extract and lemon juice. Beat for 3 minutes. The batter will be a light lemon color when done.

2. Add the all purpose flour and milk. Mix only until the **Ingredients** are incorporated. The batter will be thick. It may be easier to mix in the flour with a large wooden spoon.

3. Spray a 10" bundt pan with non stick cooking spray. Spoon the batter into the pan. Bake the cake for 1 1/4 hours or until a toothpick inserted in the center comes out clean. The cake will be light brown on the top.

4. Remove the cake from the oven and cool the cake in the pan for 10 minutes. Invert the cake onto a serving plate or a wire rack to cool. You may need to run a knife or spatula around the pan to help remove the cake. Cool the cake completely before cutting. This cake needs to rest 6-8 hours before eating to develop the flavor.

5. Note: This cake is easily over cooked and every oven bakes differently. Start checking the cake at 45 minutes to see if it is done. Keep checking every 10 minutes until the cake is done.

Coconut Pound Cake

Ingredients

- 1 cup softened unsalted butter

- 2 cups granulated sugar

- 4 eggs

- 3 tsp. coconut extract

- 3 cups all purpose flour

- 1/2 tsp. salt

- 1/2 tsp. baking soda

- 1/2 tsp. baking powder

- 1 cup whole milk

- 1 cup sweetened flaked coconut

- 1 cup chopped pecans

- Coconut Syrup recipe below

Directions

1. Preheat the oven to 325°. Spray a 10" bundt pan with non stick cooking spray. In a large bowl, add the butter and the granulated sugar. Using a mixer on medium speed, beat for 4 minutes. Add the eggs and coconut extract. Beat for 4 minutes.

2. Sift together the all purpose flour, salt, baking soda and baking powder. Reduce the mixer speed to low and add the dry **Ingredients** and milk. Turn the mixer off and stir in the coconut and the pecans.

3. Pour the batter into the prepared pan. Bake for 1 to 1 1/2 hours or until a toothpick inserted in the center of the cake comes out clean. Remove the pan from the oven and let the cake rest in the pan while you prepare the Coconut syrup.

4. Coconut syrup: In a sauce pan over medium heat, add 1 cup granulated sugar, 1/2 cup water, 2

tablespoons butter, 2 tablespoons light corn syrup and 1 teaspoon coconut extract. Stir constantly and bring the syrup to a boil. Boil for 5 minutes. Remove the pan from the heat and pour the syrup over the cake in the pan. Let the cake sit in the pan until completely cool. Invert the cake onto a serving plate when cool.

Sour Cream Pound Cake

Ingredients

- 1 cup softened unsalted butter

- 3 cups granulated sugar

- 6 eggs

- 1 tsp. vanilla extract

- 1 tsp. lemon juice

- 1 cup sour cream

- 3 cups all purpose flour

- 1/4 tsp. baking powder

- 1/2 tsp. salt

Directions

1. Preheat the oven to 325°. Spray a 10" bundt pan with non stick cooking spray. In a large mixing bowl, add the butter and granulated sugar. Using a mixer on medium speed, beat for 3 minutes. Add the eggs, vanilla extract, lemon juice and sour cream. Beat for 4 minutes. Reduce the mixer speed to low. Add the all purpose flour, baking powder and salt. Mix only until well combined. The batter will be thick.

2. Spoon the batter into the prepared pan. Bake for 1 1/4 hours or until a toothpick inserted in the center of the cake comes out clean. Remove the cake from the oven and cool the cake in the pan for 10 minutes. Carefully run a knife around the pan edges and the center to loosen the cake. Invert the pan onto a serving plate. Cool the cake completely before serving.

3. I like to make pound cakes at least 8-10 hours before serving. The flavor is always better when the cake has time to rest.

Cream Cheese Pound Cake

Ingredients

- 1 cup margarine, softened

- 1/2 cup unsalted butter, softened

- 8 oz. cream cheese, softened

- 3 cups granulated sugar

- 2 tsp. vanilla extract

- 6 eggs, at room temperature

- 3 cups all purpose flour

Directions

1. In a mixing bowl, add the margarine, butter and cream cheese. Using a mixer on medium speed, beat for 4 minutes. The mixture should be light and fluffy when ready. Add the granulated sugar, vanilla extract and eggs. Beat for 3 minutes or until the batter is smooth and combined. Add the all purpose flour and mix only until combined.

2. Set the oven to 275°. You do not preheat the oven for this cake. The cake will be put in a cold oven. Spray a 10" tube pan with non stick cooking spray. Spoon the cake batter in the pan. Bake for 1 1/2 hours or until a toothpick inserted in the center of the cake comes out clean. Remove the cake from the pan and cool the cake completely in the pan. Remove the cake from the pan and serve.

Sweet Potato Pound Cake

Ingredients

- 1 cup unsalted butter, softened

- 2 cups granulated sugar

- 4 eggs

- 2 1/2 cups cooked mashed sweet potatoes

- 3 cups all purpose flour

- 2 tsp. baking powder

- 1 tsp. baking soda

- 1 tsp. ground cinnamon

- 1/2 tsp. ground nutmeg

- 1/4 tsp. salt

- 1 tsp. vanilla extract

- 1/2 cup sweetened flaked coconut

- 1/2 cup chopped pecans

Directions

1. Preheat the oven to 350°. Spray a 10" bundt pan with non stick cooking spray. In a large mixing bowl, add the butter and granulated sugar. Using a mixer on medium speed, beat for 3 minutes. Add the eggs and beat for 3 minutes. Reduce the mixer speed to low. Add the sweet potatoes and mix

until combined.

2. Add the all purpose flour, baking powder, baking soda, cinnamon, nutmeg, salt and vanilla extract. Mix only until well combined. The batter will be thick. Turn the mixer off and fold in the coconut and pecans.

3. Spoon the batter into the prepared pan. Bake for 1 1/4 hours or until a toothpick inserted in the center of the cake comes out clean. Remove the cake from the oven and cool the cake in the pan for 10 minutes. Carefully run a knife around the pan edges and the center to loosen the cake. Invert the pan onto a serving plate. Cool the cake completely before serving.

Apple Cider Pound Cake

Ingredients

- 1 cup unsalted butter, softened
- 1/2 cup vegetable shortening
- 3 cups granulated sugar
- 6 eggs
- 3 cups all purpose flour
- 1/2 tsp. baking powder
- 1/2 tsp. salt
- 3/4 tsp. ground cinnamon
- 1/2 tsp. ground allspice
- 1/2 tsp. ground nutmeg
- 1/4 tsp. ground cloves
- 1 cup apple cider
- 1 tsp. vanilla extract

Directions

1. All **Ingredients** must be at room temperature. A great pound cake requires thorough mixing. Preheat the oven to 325°. In a large mixing bowl, add the butter and vegetable shortening. With your mixer on medium speed, beat for 3 minutes. Add the granulated sugar and beat for 4 minutes. Add the eggs and beat for 3 minutes.

2. Add the all purpose flour, baking powder, salt, cinnamon, allspice, nutmeg, cloves, apple cider and vanilla extract. Mix only until the **Ingredients** are incorporated. Spray a 10" tube pan with non stick cooking spray. Spoon the batter into the pan. Bake the cake for 1 1/2 hours or until a toothpick inserted in the center of the cake comes out clean.

3. Remove the cake from the oven and cool the cake in the pan for 10 minutes. Invert the cake onto a

serving plate or a wire rack to cool. You may need to run a knife or spatula around the pan to help remove the cake. Remove the pan from the cake and cool the cake completely before cutting.

Brandy Pound Cake

Ingredients

- 2 cups unsalted butter, softened

- 2 cups granulated sugar

- 9 eggs

- 4 cups all purpose flour

- 1/2 tsp. cream of tartar

- 1/2 tsp. salt

- 2 tbs. brandy

Directions

1. All **Ingredients** must be at room temperature. A great pound cake requires thorough mixing. Preheat the oven to 325°. In a large mixing bowl, add the butter and granulated sugar. With a mixer on medium speed, beat for 4 minutes. Add the eggs and beat for 3 minutes.

2. Add the all purpose flour, cream of tartar, salt and brandy. Mix only until the **Ingredients** are incorporated. Spray two 9 x 5 loaf pans with non stick cooking spray. Spoon the batter into the pans. Bake for 1 hour or until a toothpick inserted in the center of the cakes comes out clean.

3. Remove the cakes from the oven and cool the cakes in the pans for 10 minutes. Remove the cakes from the pans and cool completely before slicing.

Chocolate Pound Cake

Ingredients

- 1/2 cup vegetable shortening

- 1 cup plus 2 tbs. unsalted butter, softened

- 3 cups granulated sugar

- 5 eggs, at room temperature

- 3 cups all purpose flour

- 1/2 tsp. baking powder

- 1/2 tsp. salt

- 1/3 cup unsweetened baking cocoa

- 1 1/4 cups whole milk

- 1 oz. unsweetened baking chocolate

- 1 cup powdered sugar

- 2 tbs. boiling water

Directions

1. Preheat the oven to 350°. Spray a 10" bundt pan with non stick cooking spray.

2. In a large mixing bowl, add the vegetable shortening and 1 cup butter. Using a mixer on medium speed, beat for 3 minutes. Add the granulated sugar and mix for 3 minutes. Add the eggs and mix for 3 minutes. Reduce the mixer speed to low. Add the all purpose flour, baking powder, salt, unsweetened cocoa and milk. Mix only until well combined.

3. Spoon the batter into the prepared pan. Bake for 1 1/4 hours or until a toothpick inserted in the center of the cake comes out clean. Remove the cake from the oven and cool the cake for 10 minutes in the pan. Carefully run a knife around the pan edges and the center to loosen the cake. Invert the pan onto a serving plate. Remove the pan and cool completely before glazing.

4. In a small sauce pan over low heat, add 2 tablespoons butter and the baking chocolate. Stir constantly and cook until the chocolate and butter melt. Remove the pan from the heat and stir in the powdered sugar and boiling water. Stir until the glaze is smooth and combined. Drizzle the glaze over the cooled cake. Let the cake sit at room temperature for 6 hours before serving.

Mocha Pound Cake

Ingredients

- 2/3 cup vegetable shortening

- 1 1/4 cups granulated sugar

- 3 eggs

- 2 oz. semisweet chocolate, melted

- 2 tsp. instant coffee granules

- 1/2 cup water

- 2 cups sifted cake flour

- 1 tsp salt

- 1/2 tsp. cream of tartar

- 1/4 tsp. baking soda

- 1 tsp. vanilla extract

Directions

1. Preheat the oven to 325°. Spray a 9 x 5 loaf pan with non stick cooking spray. In a large mixing bowl, add the vegetable shortening and granulated sugar. Using a mixer on medium speed, beat for 4

minutes. Add the eggs and melted chocolate to the bowl. Beat for 3 minutes.

2. In a small bowl, add the coffee granules and water. Stir until the coffee dissolves. Add the coffee to the mixing bowl. Add the cake flour, salt, cream of tartar, baking soda and vanilla extract. Mix until the batter is smooth and combined.

3. Spoon the batter into the loaf pan. Bake for 1 hour or until a toothpick inserted in the center of the cake comes out clean. Remove the cake from the oven and cool the cake in the pan for 10 minutes. Remove the cake from the pan and cool completely before cutting.

Pecan Topped Chocolate Pound Cake

Ingredients

- 1 cup unsalted butter, softened
- 1/2 cup vegetable shortening
- 2 1/2 cups granulated sugar
- 5 eggs
- 3 cups all purpose flour
- 1/2 cup unsweetened baking cocoa
- 1 cup whole milk
- 1 cup chopped pecans

Directions

1. All **Ingredients** must be at room temperature. A great pound cake requires thorough mixing. Preheat the oven to 325°. In a large mixing bowl, add the butter and vegetable shortening. Using a mixer on medium speed, beat the butter and shortening for 3 minutes. Add the granulated sugar and beat for 4 minutes. Add the eggs and beat for 3 minutes.

2. Add the all purpose flour, cocoa and milk. Mix only until the **Ingredients** are incorporated. Spray a 10" tube pan with non stick cooking spray. Spoon the batter into the pan. Sprinkle the pecans over the top of the cake batter. Bake for 1 1/4 hours or until a toothpick inserted in the center of the cake comes out clean.

3. Remove the cake from the oven and cool the cake in the pan for 15 minutes. Invert the cake onto a serving plate or a wire rack to cool. You may need to run a knife or spatula around the pan to help remove the cake. Remove the pan from the cake and cool the cake completely before cutting. Place the cake on a serving platter with the pecan side up.

Buttermilk Pound Cake

Ingredients

- 1/2 cup unsalted butter, softened

- 1/2 cup vegetable shortening

- 2 cups granulated sugar

- 4 eggs, at room temperature

- 1/2 tsp. baking soda

- 1 cup buttermilk

- 3 cups all purpose flour

- 1/8 tsp. salt

- 2 tsp. lemon extract

- 1 tsp. almond extract

Directions

1. All **Ingredients** must be at room temperature. A great pound cake requires thorough mixing. Preheat the oven to 350°. In a large mixing bowl, add the butter and vegetable shortening. With a mixer on medium speed, beat for 3 minutes. Add the granulated sugar and beat for 4 minutes. Add the eggs and beat for 3 minutes.

2. Add the baking soda, buttermilk, all purpose flour, salt, lemon extract and almond extract. Mix only until the **Ingredients** are incorporated. Spray a 10" tube pan with non stick cooking spray. Spoon the batter into the pan. Bake the cake for 1 1/4 hours or until a toothpick inserted in the center of the cake comes out clean.

3. Remove the cake from the oven and cool the cake in the pan for 10 minutes. Invert the cake onto a serving plate or a wire rack to cool. You may need to run a knife or spatula around the pan to help remove the cake. Remove the pan from the cake and cool the cake completely before cutting.

Brown Sugar Pound Cake

Ingredients

- 1 cup vegetable shortening

- 3/4 cup unsalted butter, softened

- 4 cups light brown sugar

- 5 eggs

- 3 cups all purpose flour

- 1/2 tsp. salt

- 1/2 tsp. baking powder

- 1 cup evaporated milk

- 2 tsp. maple flavoring

- 1 1/2 cups powdered sugar

- 2 tbs. whole milk

- 1/2 tsp. vanilla extract

Directions

1. All **Ingredients** must be at room temperature. A great pound cake requires thorough mixing. Preheat the oven to 325°. In a large mixing bowl, add 1/2 cup butter and vegetable shortening. Using a mixer on medium speed, beat for 3 minutes. Add 3 1/2 cups brown sugar and beat for 4 minutes. Add the eggs and beat for 3 minutes.

2. Add the all purpose flour, salt, baking powder, evaporated milk and maple flavoring. Mix only until the **Ingredients** are well blended. Spray a 10" tube pan with non stick cooking spray. Spoon the batter into the pan. Bake the cake for 1 1/4 hours or until a toothpick inserted in the center of the cake comes out clean.

3. Remove the cake from the oven and cool the cake in the pan for 10 minutes. Invert the cake onto a serving plate or a wire rack to cool. You may need to run a knife or spatula around the pan to help remove the cake. Remove the pan from the cake and cool the cake completely before frosting.

4. In a sauce pan over medium heat, add 1/4 cup butter, powdered sugar, 1/2 cup brown sugar, whole milk and vanilla extract. Stir constantly and cook until the butter and sugars melt. The icing should be smooth and combined. Remove the pan from the heat and spoon over the top of the cooled pound cake.

Bourbon Pecan Pound Cake

Ingredients

- 1 cup vegetable shortening

- 2 1/2 cups granulated sugar

- 6 eggs, at room temperature

- 3 cups all purpose flour

- 2 tsp. baking powder

- 1/2 tsp. salt

- 1/2 tsp. ground nutmeg

- 1 cup sour cream

- 1/2 cup plus 2 tbs. bourbon

- 1 cup finely chopped pecans

- 2 1/4 cups powdered sugar

- 2 tbs. water

Directions

1. Preheat the oven to 325°. In a mixing bowl, add the vegetable shortening and granulated sugar. Using a mixer on medium speed, beat for 4 minutes. Add the eggs and beat for 4 minutes. Add the all purpose flour, baking powder, salt, nutmeg, sour cream and 1/2 cup bourbon. Mix only until the batter is smooth and combined. Turn the mixer off and stir in the pecans.

2. Spoon the batter into the prepared pan. Bake for 1 1/4 hours or until a toothpick inserted in the center of the cake comes out clean. Remove the cake from the oven and cool the cake in the pan for 10 minutes. Invert the cake onto a serving plate and cool the cake completely before glazing.

3. To make the glaze, add 2 tablespoons bourbon, powdered sugar and water. Whisk until the glaze is smooth and combined. Drizzle the glaze over the top of the cake. Let the cake sit for 6 hours before serving.

Blueberry Pound Cake

Ingredients

- 1 cup plus 2 tbs. unsalted butter, softened

- 2 1/4 cups granulated sugar

- 4 eggs

- 1 tsp. vanilla extract

- 3 cups all purpose flour

- 1 tsp. baking powder

- 1/2 tsp. salt

- 2 cups fresh blueberries

Directions

1. Grease a 10" tube pan with 2 tablespoons butter. Sprinkle 1/4 cup sugar over the butter. Preheat the oven to 325°. In a mixing bowl, add 1 cup butter and 2 cups granulated sugar. Using a mixer on medium speed, beat for 3 minutes. Add the eggs and vanilla extract. Beat for 4 minutes.

2. Add 2 3/4 cups all purpose flour, baking powder and salt. Mix only until combined. In a small bowl, add 1/4 cup all purpose flour and the blueberries. Toss until the blueberries are coated in the flour. Turn the mixer off and fold in the blueberries.

3. Spoon the batter into the prepared pan. Bake for 1 hour or until a toothpick inserted in the center of the cake comes out clean. Remove the cake from the oven and cool the cake in the pan for 10 minutes. Invert the cake onto a serving plate and cool the cake for 8 hours before serving.

Cake Mix Lemon Pound Cake

Ingredients

- 4 eggs

- 18 oz. box yellow cake mix

- 4 serving size pkg. instant lemon pudding mix

- 3/4 cup water

- 1/3 cup vegetable oil

- 2 cups powdered sugar

- 1/3 cup lemon juice

Directions

1. Preheat the oven to 350°. In a mixing bowl, add the eggs. Using a mixer on medium speed, beat for 4 minutes. Add the cake mix, dry lemon pudding mix, water and vegetable oil. Beat for 8 minutes.

2. Spoon the batter into a 10" ungreased tube pan with removable bottom. Bake for 50 minutes or until a toothpick inserted in the center of the cake comes out clean. Remove the cake from the oven. Run a knife around the sides of the cake to loosen the cake from the pan. Remove the sides from the cake leaving the bottom part of the pan attached.

3. In a small sauce pan over medium heat, add the powdered sugar and lemon juice. Stir constantly and bring the glaze to a boil. Remove the pan from the heat. Using a fork, poke holes in the cake. Drizzle the hot glaze over the cake. Cool the cake completely before serving.

4. You can use virtually any flavor pudding mix instead of the lemon pudding mix. For chocolate pound cake, substitute chocolate pudding for the lemon and 1/3 cup melted chocolate for the lemon juice in the glaze. If using other flavor pudding mixes, omit the glaze or use your favorite powdered sugar glaze.

Lemon Pound Cake

Ingredients

- 1 1/4 cups unsalted butter, softened

- 1/2 cup vegetable shortening

- 3 cups granulated sugar

- 5 eggs, at room temperature

- 1 tbs. grated lemon zest

- 1 tbs. plus 1 tsp. lemon extract

- 3 cups all purpose flour

- 1 tsp. salt

- 1/2 tsp. baking powder

- 1 cup whole milk

- 1 3/4 cups powdered sugar

- 2 tbs. lemon juice

Directions

1. A great pound cake requires thorough mixing. Preheat the oven to 350°. In a large mixing bowl, add 1 cup butter and the vegetable shortening. Using a mixer on medium speed, beat for 3 minutes. Add the granulated sugar and beat for 2 minutes. Add the eggs, lemon zest and 1 tablespoon lemon extract. Beat for 3 minutes. The batter will be light and smooth. Add the all purpose flour, salt, baking powder and milk to the batter. Mix only until combined.

2. Spray a 10" bundt or tube pan with non stick cooking spray. Spoon the batter into the pan scraping the bowl to remove all the batter. Bake for 1 hour and ten minutes or until a toothpick inserted in the center of the cake comes out clean. Remove the cake from the oven and cool the cake in the pan for 10 minutes. Invert the cake onto a serving plate. Cool the cake completely before frosting.

3. In a mixing bowl, add 1/4 cup butter, powdered sugar, lemon juice and 1 teaspoon lemon extract. Using a mixer on medium speed, beat until smooth and combined. Spoon the frosting around the top of the cake allowing the frosting to slightly drip down the sides of the cake. Let the cake rest for 2 hours before serving.

Orange Juice Bundt Cake

Ingredients

- 18 oz. box yellow cake mix

- 4 serving size pkg. lemon jello

- 2/3 cup water

- 2/3 cup vegetable oil

- 4 eggs

- 1 cup orange juice

- 1/2 cup granulated sugar

Directions

1. Preheat the oven to 350°. Spray a 10" bundt pan with non stick cooking spray. In a large mixing bowl, add the cake mix, dry lemon jello, water, vegetable oil and eggs. Using a mixer on medium speed, beat for 4 minutes.

2. Pour the batter into the prepared pan. Bake for 35 minutes or until a toothpick inserted in the center of the cake comes out clean. Remove the cake from the oven.

3. In a small bowl, combine the orange juice and granulated sugar. Pour the juice over the hot cake. Cool the cake completely in the pan. When the cake is cool, invert the cake onto a serving plate.

Orange Jello Cake

Ingredients

- 18 oz. box orange cake mix
- 4 serving size pkg. orange jello
- 3/4 cup water
- 3/4 cup vegetable oil
- 4 eggs
- 2 tbs. lemon juice
- 1/2 - 1 cup powdered sugar

Directions

1. Preheat the oven to 350°. Spray a 10" bundt pan with non stick cooking spray. In a large mixing bowl, add the cake mix, dry orange jello, water, vegetable oil and eggs. Using a mixer on medium speed, beat for 4 minutes.

2. Pour the batter into the prepared pan. Bake for 35 minutes or until a toothpick inserted in the center of the cake comes out clean. Remove the cake from the oven and cool the cake in the pan for 10 minutes. Remove the cake from the pan and place on a serving platter.

3. While the cake is still warm, prepare the glaze. In a small bowl, add the lemon juice and 1/2 cup powdered sugar. Mix together until you have a pourable but thick glaze. Add the remaining powdered sugar if needed to make the glaze consistency. Pour the glaze over the cake while the cake is still warm.

Punch Bowl Cake

Ingredients

- 18 oz. box yellow cake mix
- 2 cans cherry pie filling, 21 oz. size
- 4 boxes instant vanilla pudding mix, 4 serving size
- 8 cups whole milk
- 15 oz. can pineapple tidbits
- 4 bananas, peeled and sliced
- 2 tbs. lemon juice
- 16 oz. carton Cool Whip, thawed
- 1/2 cup chopped pecans

- 1/2 cup maraschino cherries

- 1/2 cup sweetened flaked coconut

Directions

1. Prepare and bake the cake mix according to package **Directions**. Bake the cake in two 9" round cake pans. Cool the cake completely before using. Cut the cake into cubes.

2. In a large punch bowl, add half the cake cubes. Spread 1 can cherry pie filling over the cake. In a mixing bowl, add the vanilla pudding mix and milk. Using a mixer on medium speed, beat until the pudding thickens. Spread half the pudding over the cherry pie filling. Spread half the pineapple over the pudding.

3. In a mixing bowl, add the bananas and lemon juice. Toss until the bananas are coated in the lemon juice. Spread half the bananas over the pineapple. Spread half the Cool Whip over the top. Repeat the layering process one more time using the remaining cake, cherry pie filling, pudding, pineapple, bananas and Cool Whip. Sprinkle the pecans, maraschino cherries and coconut over the top. Cover the top of the punch bowl and refrigerate at least 8 hours before serving.

Cherry Topped Flourless Chocolate Cake

Ingredients

- 5 tsp. unsweetened cocoa

- 1 cup unsalted butter, cubed

- 9 oz. semisweet baking chocolate, chopped

- 5 eggs

- 1/2 cup plus 1 tbs. granulated sugar

- 2 tsp. vanilla extract

- 21 oz. can cherry pie filling

- 1 cup Cool Whip, thawed

Directions

1. Spray a 9" springform pan with non stick cooking spray. Line the entire pan waxed paper. Spray the waxed paper with non stick cooking spray. Sprinkle 2 teaspoons unsweetened cocoa over the waxed paper. Wrap the outside of the pan twice with heavy duty aluminum foil. Make sure the bottom of the pan is wrapped.

2. In a sauce pan over low heat, add the butter and semisweet chocolate. Stir constantly and cook until the chocolate and butter melt. Remove the pan from the heat and cool until the chocolate is lukewarm.

3. In a large mixing bowl, add the eggs and 1/2 cup granulated sugar. Using a mixer on medium speed, beat for 4 minutes. The eggs should be light and lemon colored when ready. Add 3 teaspoons cocoa,

1 tablespoon granulated sugar and vanilla extract to the bowl. Mix until well combined. Add the cooled chocolate and mix until combined. Spoon the batter into the prepared pan.

4. Place the pan in a roasting pan. Pour hot water about 3/4" up the sides of the springform pan. Preheat the oven to 325°. Bake for 35 minutes or until a toothpick inserted off center of the cake comes out clean. Remove the cake from the oven and immediately remove the cake from the roasting pan. Cool the cake for 20 minutes in the springform pan.

5. Run a knife around the edges of the pan and remove the cake from the pan. Cool the cake completely before topping. Spread the cherry pie filling over the top of the cake. Spread the Cool Whip over the cherry pie filling and serve.

Popcorn Cake

Ingredients

- 4 qts. popped popcorn
- 8 oz. dry salted peanuts
- 1 lb. small gumdrops
- 1/2 cup unsalted butter
- 1/2 cup vegetable oil
- 1 lb. marshmallows
- Colored sprinkles

Directions

1. In a large bowl, add the popcorn, peanuts and gumdrops. In a microwavable bowl, add the butter. Microwave for 30 seconds or until the butter melts. Remove the bowl from the microwave. Add the vegetable oil and marshmallows to the butter. Stir until the marshmallows are melted. Microwave for 10-15 seconds if needed to melt the marshmallows.

2. Pour the syrup over the popcorn in the bowl. Blend the mixture with your hands. The syrup should not be so hot that you will get a burn. Mix until well combined.

3. Spray a 10 cup angel food pan or tube pan with non stick cooking spray. Scoop the popcorn mixture into the pan. Press down and make sure the popcorn is compressed into the pan.

4. Sprinkle the cake with as many sprinkles as desired. Let the cake sit for 1 hour in the pan. Run a knife around the edges of the pan. Invert the cake onto a serving plate. Place the cake, sprinkle side up, on a serving platter. Cut into slices and serve.

Lemon Apricot Cake

Ingredients

- 18 oz. box lemon cake mix

- 1 cup apricot nectar

- 1/4 cup vegetable oil

- 4 eggs

- 1/2 cup granulated sugar

- 2 cups powdered sugar

- 2-3 tbs. lemon juice

Directions

1. Preheat the oven to 350°. In a large mixing bowl, add the cake mix, apricot nectar, vegetable oil, eggs and granulated sugar. Using a mixer on medium speed, beat for 4 minutes. The batter should be smooth and well combined.

2. Spray y1 10" bundt pan with non stick cooking spray. Spoon the batter into the pan. Bake for 40 minutes or until a knife inserted in the center of the cake comes out clean. Remove the cake from the oven.

3. Let the cake rest in the pan for 10 minutes. Run a knife around the edges and center of the pan if needed to loosen the cake. Invert the pan onto a serving plate. Leave the bundt pan on the cake until it falls out of the pan. If you sprayed your pan well, it should fall right out. Cool the cake completely before glazing.

4. For the glaze, add the powdered sugar and 2 tablespoons lemon juice to a small bowl. Whisk until combined. Add the remaining juice if needed to thin the glaze. Drizzle the glaze over the cooled cake.

Blackberry Loaf Cake

Ingredients

- 1/2 cup unsalted butter

- 1 cup granulated sugar

- 3 eggs

- 1 1/2 cups all purpose flour

- 2 tsp. baking powder

- 1/2 tsp. ground nutmeg

- 1/2 tsp. ground cinnamon

- 1/2 cup whole milk

- 1 tsp. lemon juice

- 1 cup fresh blackberries, washed

Directions

1. Preheat the oven to 350°. Spray a 9 x 5 loaf pan with non stick cooking spray. In a mixing bowl, add the butter and granulated sugar. Using a mixer on medium speed, beat for 3 minutes. Add the eggs and beat for 3 minutes. Add 1 cup all purpose flour, baking powder, nutmeg, cinnamon and milk. Mix only until combined. Add the lemon juice and mix until combined.

2. In a small bowl, add 1/2 cup all purpose flour and the blackberries. Toss until the blackberries are coated in the flour. Turn the mixer off and fold in the blackberries. Spoon the batter into the prepared pan.

3. Bake for 1 hour or until a toothpick inserted in the center of the cake comes out clean. Remove the cake from the oven and cool in the pan for 10 minutes. Remove the cake from the pan and cool for 10 minutes. Serve the cake warm or at room temperature.

Whiskey Cake

Ingredients

- 1/2 cup unsalted butter, softened
- 1 cup granulated sugar
- 3 eggs
- 1 cup all purpose flour
- 1/2 tsp. baking powder
- 1/4 tsp. salt
- 1/2 tsp. ground nutmeg
- 1/4 cup whole milk
- 1/4 cup molasses
- 1/4 tsp. baking soda
- 1/4 cup bourbon
- 2 cups raisins
- 2 cups chopped pecans

Directions

1. Preheat the oven to 300°. Spray a 9 x 5 loaf pan with non stick cooking spray. In a mixing bowl, add the butter and granulated sugar. Using a mixer on medium speed, beat for 3 minutes. Add the eggs and beat for 3 minutes. Add the all purpose flour, baking powder, salt, nutmeg and milk. Mix only until combined.

2. In a small bowl, add the molasses and baking soda. Stir until combined and add to the cake batter. Mix until combined. Turn off the mixer and stir in the bourbon, raisins and pecans. Spoon the batter

into the prepared pan.

3. Bake for 1 1/2 hours or until a toothpick inserted in the center of the cake comes out clean. Remove the cake from the oven and cool in the pan for 10 minutes. Remove the cake from the pan and cool completely before serving. You can refrigerate the cake until chilled for easier slicing.